Five Secrets That Will Triple Your Profits!

By T.J. Rohleder,
Co-Founder of M.O.R.E. Incorporated
&
Founder of the Direct-Response Network

TABLE OF CONTENTS

INTRODUCTION

by T.J. Rohleder

"Little hinges swing big doors."

Congratulations on your decision to read this book. After all, most businesspeople and entrepreneurs 'claim' they want to make more money, but how many are willing to pick up and study a book that can help them do it? I'm ashamed to say that the answer is very few.

Yes, most people want all of the benefits <u>without</u> paying the price to get them. Earl Nightingale called this *"the strangest secret"* and recorded one of the first audio programs over 50 years ago to describe this phenomenon... Unfortunately, this is even a bigger problem today than it was when Earl recorded his classic program. Nowadays it seems as if almost everyone is looking for a free ride or something for nothing. Very few people are willing to pay the price to get what they want. *This is bad news for them...*

But it's great news for YOU!

Why? That's simple. You see, the people who are unwilling to do whatever it takes to build their business includes <u>most</u> of your competitors. Because of this, you can dramatically gain an almost unfair advantage over all of these individuals and companies. This book shows you how. You can use the Secrets inside the five chapters of this book to...

Become a dominant competitor in your market and start getting all of the money that could and should be yours.

The five secrets in this book really are *'secrets'* because most of your competitors don't know about them. As you'll see, each of these secrets is easy to understand and simple to use. There's nothing complicated about any of this. But don't let this simplicity fool you. Even though these secrets are simple to understand and easy to use, each one really does have the awesome power to make you huge sums of money. And together...

All five of these secrets will create a synergistic force that lets you GAIN AN UNFAIR ADVANTAGE over all of your competitors!

So don't let the size of this small book fool you. You see, *"Little hinges really do swing big doors."* The five marketing secrets in this book truly can triple your profits in no time flat! Using all five of these secrets will help you quickly attract and retain more customers within your market area. That's what marketing is all about, by the way.

The word *marketing* is thrown around a lot these days and used rather loosely... **But my definition is so simple a grade school kid can understand it.** Here it is:

"Marketing is made up of all the things you do to attract and sell to the right people who are perfectly suited for whatever you offer — and then all the things you do to re-sell as much as you can to these people (and perhaps their closest contacts) for as many years as possible."

This clear definition tells you _exactly_ what you must do:

A: Attract the right prospective buyers to your business.

B: Then re-sell to them (and perhaps their closest associates) for as many months and years as possible.

Forget the complicated theories. Good marketing is simply **attracting and retaining the right kind of customers — who will do the largest amount of repeat business with you** over the longest period of time. (Why more college business schools don't teach this will always be a mystery to me.)

So that's our definition of marketing. Simple. Clear. Direct. There's no confusion here. In fact, there's nothing complicated about any of this. You see, building a business is actually a very simple process... There are only three ways to do it:

#1: You can increase the number of new customers who are attracted to your business.

#2: You can increase the frequency of repeat business these people do with you (in other words, you can do things to get them to re-buy more often).

#3: You can increase the average profit of each repeat transaction you do with your ever-growing base of customers.

THE FIVE MARKETING SECRETS in this book can be applied to all three of these business building areas. Do this and you will see dramatic improvements right away... Then within 90 days or so — your take-home profits can be double or tripple what they are now!

Still sound unbelievable? If so, that's okay. But please study this book carefully and prove to yourself that this is true. Just spend some time thinking about all of the ways that you can use these five key secrets. Spend some time doing this every day and let these five very simple, but powerful secrets help you triple your profits in no time flat.

And to reward you for reading this book, I have...

A great FREE business-building gift for you!

Yes, I have a gift waiting for you that can help you make huge sums of extra money! Here's what it's all about: Throughout this small book are 40 additional marketing secrets that came from a special eBook I have just written, called; *"265 of the Greatest Marketing Secrets You Can Use to Dominate Your Market."* This Electronic Book is on the Internet and ready for you to download right now! It normally sells for $27.95 — and is worth every penny. But for a limited time it can be yours — absolutely FREE — by simply going to my Web-Site and giving me your contact information.

Why am I giving you this $27.95 eBook for free? That's simple. You see, I have other products and services that were developed to help you make the maximum amount of money that I would love to tell you about. So I'm more than happy to give you this brand new Electronic Book that gives you 265 of my greatest marketing secrets if you'll give me your contact information (which I will not give out to anyone). IT'S EASY TO RECEIVE THIS FREE GIFT: just go to **www.RuthlessMarketing.com/FreeGift** and immediately download this very special Electronic Marketing book. And don't worry, although I <u>will</u> add your name to my mailing list and send you additional information, there is NEVER any cost or obligation for you to purchase anything else from me, now or in the future. This FREE gift will be my way of thanking you for taking the time to read and study this book.

So with all this said, let's begin...

Establishing Your USP

In this chapter, we're going to talk about building a Unique Selling Position — what's also known in the industry as a Unique Selling Proposition or, more succinctly, a USP. If you have no idea what a USP is, then what you learn in this chapter alone will be worth every penny you paid for this book. Even if you already know all about USPs, by the time we're done here you'll have learned a lot you didn't know already, and you'll have supercharged your understanding of this valuable marketing strategy.

Ask yourself this one question as you read this chapter: why do your clients buy from you instead of your competitors? If you can't answer that question, it means one of two things: either you're offering your clients a unique set of advantages that you've never bothered to identify, or you offer *no* unique advantages, so you're lucky to have any business in the first place. If that's the case, there's no compelling reason for your customers to keep doing business with you. Therefore, **anytime your competitors offer your customers a unique advantage, they can steal those customers away.**

You can't let that happen! In this chapter, I'm going to show you how to build your own Unique Selling Position: a USP that completely separates you from all of the other competitors in your market, and makes people want to keep doing business with you over and over again. So, please: read carefully, and take plenty of notes.

What a USP Is, and Why It's Important

Ask a dozen marketing experts what a USP is, and you'll get

a dozen answers — but they'll have a lot in common. At its most basic, a USP is **a clear statement of the unique benefits your customers get from doing business with you. It's something that sets you apart from your competition.** No matter what field you're in, all your competitors are usually saying the same thing. A USP is something — a benefit, an idea, a concept — that helps you say something your competitors don't, so that when people look at your business, it stands out against the rest of the field and looks unique to their eyes.

The most unique USP possible would be to have a product that everybody wants and nobody else has. The only problem there is that 99.99% of businesses *don't* have that. They've got plenty of competition. It doesn't matter if you're a chiropractor, a dentist, an attorney, a plumber, or an air conditioner repairman: whatever you're doing, chances are you've got competition up the kazoo. A USP is important because it defines you and your company, and gives potential customers a very compelling reason — or even several reasons — why they should favor you over all those competitors.

You can **look at a USP as simply what you do better or differently than everybody else. In most cases, you should be able to get your USP down to a few words.** Here are three great examples I picked up from a website. Burger King

---

says, "Have it your way!" Enterprise Car Rental says, "We'll pick you up." Bounty Paper Towels call themselves "The Quicker Picker-Upper." The best USP is a condensed catchphrase that tells your customers why they should do business with you instead of your competition. Your answer has to telegraph a very clear and direct benefit to your prospect or customer, in a concise, distinct, fulfilling way.

For example, if you were to say, "Melts in your mouth, not in your hands!" everyone would know you were talking about M & M's. That's a classic USP, and it's sold millions of dollars worth of candy over the years. A good USP like that one stays with a person, etched into both their subconscious and their conscious mind, so when they walk away and later think about buying a product in that particular category, they'll think of you first. Here are a few more great examples: take Avis Rent-A-Car. They couldn't be #1 in their market — that was Hertz — so they came up with this USP: "We're #2. We try harder!" And here's Federal Express: "When it absolutely, positively has to be get there overnight." And then there's the old USP for Domino's Pizza, which is my favorite, though the government actually court-ordered them to stop using it because of a lawsuit. It was so brilliant: "Fresh hot pizza in 30 minutes or less!" What could be clearer than that?

The USP, then, is whatever you can offer that your best prospects or customers want the most that nobody else has — and it's up to you to discover or create that. I'm going to show you how in this chapter. But just as important, I'm going to show you exactly what a USP is *not*. If you flip through the Yellow Pages or a newspaper advertising section, you'll see plenty of examples of what a USP is not: and that's just your name, your address, your telephone number, how many years you've been in business, the fact that you're "family-owned," and so on. That's what you see in most advertising — but that's not a USP. It doesn't telegraph any benefit. You need to give people not what they *need*, but what they *want*. And **what people want is to solve their problems or to fulfill their desires, as quickly, easily, and painlessly as possible.**

Taming the Wild USP

Now we'll get into the meat-and-potatoes of what a USP really is, and how to find the one that's right for you. This isn't an easy process for the inexperienced marketer. First of all, how do you get started? That's usually a little daunting, because you may not be sure exactly what a USP is, although you should have some general idea by now. **The first question you should always ask yourself is, "What needs are going unfulfilled in my industry, or in this segment of my target market? What problems need to be fixed?" The second question is, "What great value, service, or benefit will people receive from my business that will justify them doing business with me?"**

So… is a USP a slogan? It is indeed, in its most basic sense, but even then you have to gather together all your raw material before you try to put it into a statement. An easy way to do that is to compile a Claims Matrix. A Claims Matrix is a chart, a visual representation of what's out there, who's saying what, and what's available. Frankly, very few companies are in a position so unique that they don't have direct competition. Even if you have a unique service that everybody needs and no one else provides…well, you're a very rare bird, and you won't be in that position for very long. If you're trying something new, it's either going to succeed because of its uniqueness, or you're going to discover that the product is unique because there was no demand for it in the first place. Even if you do succeed, you'll have imitators very quickly. Imitation may be the sincerest form of flattery, but it can hurt you severely if it steals away dollars that should be yours.

Here's how you create a Claims Matrix to get all the raw data to work from. You can do it on paper, on a computer spreadsheet, or even in your head if you can handle all the data that way. Down one side of the chart, list all the benefits and features you can think of that pertain to your product or service. Include all the features and benefits your competition is claiming. That might be that they have 24 stores and locations, free delivery, same-day service, or whatever. You should include as many as you can think of.

Then, across the top of the chart, write the names of all your competitors. Once you've done that, go down the chart and put a checkmark next to each feature or claim that's being made by each competitor. So, if it's fast delivery and there are three competitors who make that claim, you put the checkmark in the spaces for those three businesses. Go right on down the line, and spend a little while doing this. You'd better come back after a day or so, because more features and benefits will dawn on you. When you complete this simple task, you'll have a visual representation of what other people are doing, and you'll very likely see big, open spaces where no competitor is making a claim. These open spaces offer a whole list of ideas you can claim; they're the raw data you can work from to create your own USPs. And don't be scared to have more than one, especially if you have different divisions within your company.

Here's one of the prime lessons you should take away from this chapter: *even if you're not unique, you can be unique in saying what no one else is saying.* Once you've put together a nice list of benefits and features, you can translate any of those features into additional benefits.

As you go down that list, you'll read a feature and ask yourself, "So what?" For instance, here's a typical claim: "We have the most locations." So what? "Well, that means you're never more than ten minutes away from one of our stores." So what? "That means you're only 20 minutes from having food at home that's still hot and fresh." Aha! There's your *real* benefit.

Keep going down the list. Suppose someone claims, "We have the largest inventory." So what? He has the biggest selection; what does that mean? "That means you can always find the hard-to-find items that the other stores don't carry." *Now* you have a clue.

The right marriage between message to market — the closer marriage — the more money Formula

a. Right message/offer

b. To right market

c. Through the right media

Once you complete your Claims Matrix, you have the raw data to begin crafting your USP. Your list can be very long in the beginning, but then you can start editing it down until you end up with a single statement that says everything you want to say. It tells the customer, "Here's why you should do business with me; this is a unique benefit you'll get." You're claiming something in the marketplace that none of your competition is claiming. That will help you get started. This is an ongoing process, and it may take you a few days just to get some preliminary ideas about what you want to do. But that's okay; this is something you need to hammer out right now before you even open your doors. Figure out what your point of difference is going to be. What are you going to offer to your customers and prospects that's different from everybody else? You've got to answer this question, and it has to be something that will compel them to do business with you rather than your competitors. That said, keep in mind that a USP isn't necessarily set in stone. It evolves; you're constantly asking yourself these questions, so your USP is a process rather than a static thing that just pops into your head full-grown and never changes. **Your best ideas will come from the time you put into process.**

Here's one of the things that makes this process so useful: if you talk to most businesspeople about developing a Claims Matrix and adding up all the benefits and features, they'll look at you like you're speaking a foreign language. That's because hardly anybody puts in the effort to do this, or even knows they should. This is your real advantage here. It's your edge in the marketplace: the fact that most people won't take the time to do this.

The best evidence of that is that most businesses are saying the same thing — they're "me too" businesses. Drive through any town, and you'll see hundreds of little businesses. Not that there's anything wrong with that, but these little businesses are all the same: little gift shops, hole-in-the-wall restaurants, antique stores, and the like. It's obvious that so many people have poured their hearts, lives, and all their assets into opening a business, without ever wondering how that business is going to succeed. They do no market research; they have no idea why people would do business with them, as opposed to all the other shops that are offering the same thing. They just open their doors and say, "I offer that, too."

You've also got to take care to avoid marketing pitfalls in creating your USP. Let's say you decide to carve out a niche in the printer cartridge industry. It's a very competitive market, so you might decide to build your USP around your price. Here's where you have to be careful, because the prices are more or less the same throughout the industry for specific printer cartridges. Quality? That's about the same, too. Delivery? Yep, that's about the same. So how do you differentiate yourself? How do you create a USP that gives you that competitive advantage? One individual did this: he sent out an email reminder when it was about time to replace a cartridge one of his customers had purchased.

There's always something there that research will uncover if you do it correctly, especially if you do your matrix chart first. Often, business owners and marketers talk about the benefits to the buyer, but we fail to appreciate that the important part is taking that feature and showing the customer how buying a product conveys the benefit to them. That's what your USP does. It takes the person from asking, "Should I or shouldn't I buy this product?" to a point where they say, "I can't live without this product, because it benefits me *this* way."

You May Think That's a USP, But It's Not

Wanna know a secret? Here it is: *You only have to be a little better than everybody else in order to get all the business you can handle.* One reason is that most businesses out there don't have a clue what a USP is, let alone *have* one. I'd say at least 98% of businesses out there, in any field, have no real understanding of the concept of the USP. They're not telegraphing any benefits to their prospects or customers. They hang a sign in the window that says "OPEN," and feel that's a compelling enough reason to get people stampeding through the doors. It just doesn't happen.

In order to understand what truly comprises a USP, you need to understand what a USP isn't. When I look at the ads in the newspaper, the Yellow Pages, and other venues — even the mail — I see advertisers talking about quality and service. Here's a common refrain: "We offer exceptional quality and service!" Well, holy-moly, that's going to make me run down and buy everything you have! Yeah, right. Frankly, **in most cases "quality" and "service" are empty words. They're repeated over and over by so many businesses that they've become meaningless to the consumer.** It's too often the case that the businesses using these empty words just aren't delivering on their promises. And here's the kicker: often the employees of those businesses have no idea what the company's USP is, so they don't even realize they aren't delivering on their promises. They're totally clueless — totally disconnected from the USP.

That's not to say that simple things like quality, price, and service can't make good USPs; they can, but you have to use them very, very carefully. Because they're so simple, they're often weak,

FREE GIFT: Go to www.RuthlessMarketing.com/freegift

and present hazards that can kill a young business. Here's a great USP, *if* you can back it up: your price is the lowest. It's a dangerous USP, too, because if your price is the lowest, your profit margin is small, and that may hurt you. You can only make it with this USP if you have a product that you really can cut the price on, so you can cut down the competition along with your price. This works like magic if it's still profitable. McDonald's does it with burgers, and Wal-Mart does it with discount consumer goods. Most of us can't make a dangerous USP like this work, and I'll tell you why later on.

High quality is also good USP material, but you have to explain, exactly, everything that people want to know about the quality. You can't just use those empty words I mentioned before. Greater choice can be a USP, but only if you really do have a tremendous selection. **Exceptional service is always a good USP, as long as you define your service and make it known exactly what it is you're offering.** In other words, if you offer help after the sale, you tell your customers, "Here's what we'll do for you after the sale, and how we'll be there to help you if anything comes up." A superior guarantee can be a powerful USP, but it should be a long guarantee, without a lot of escape clauses, that people can readily see is advantageous to them.

Danger, Will Robinson!

Quality, price, and service: these are all USPs that are viable, but they're weak. That is, they can work under certain circumstances, but you really, really have to know what you're doing to use them well. **In my opinion, lowest price is absolutely the worst of all the workable USPs you can try.** I'm speaking from experience here, because 20 years ago, when I started my first business, that was my USP: I was a cheap date. I was the lowest-priced provider in my market — and I'm telling you, it's horrible.

First of all, any idiot can offer the lowest price. It takes no imagination whatsoever; it takes no creativity. It's dumb for a lot

Overview of a successful marketing campaign...

a. Take the best sales points and "schemes" that have worked before...

b. Find new ways to hook them together... new themes, new angles

c. Then smooth it out... So it sounds new and different.

of reasons, but part of the reason it's dumb is that with all of the unforeseen costs in business, you need to charge premium rates just so you can afford to develop the kind of infrastructure that's needed to support the levels of service that keep your customers coming back. In my case, I was the lowest-priced carpet cleaner in my market. I couldn't afford to upgrade my equipment. My level of service was poor, because I was always running from one job to the next, and my whole business model required me to spend as little time at each job as possible. So everything suffered.

Here's another reason that offering the absolute rock-bottom lowest price is a bad idea, short and to the point: it can backfire on you. Some people will choose a product or service on price, and that's always the way they're going to shop — period. But **if they're willing to buy on price, they'll leave you on price, too.** Others shop on price because they don't know any better. The first question they ask when they call a new company is what the price is, because they don't know any other question to ask. Most businesses can't give them a better question to ask, because they don't operate with a USP.

I can't emphasize enough how important a USP is to your business. While it's true that most people shop according to price at least occasionally, they're often willing to choose goods and services based on benefits. If you can provide a USP that gives your prospect a reason to do business with you instead of the low-priced guy, they're going to choose you. **With a strong USP, you can easily justify higher prices and get them, because you're not competing on price: you've got other things to offer.** The cream is going to rise to the top: you're going to get better customers who are easier to deal with, who have money and are willing to spend it, if you offer things that appeal to those customers.

Build It, and They Will Come

In this section, I'm going to tell you how to built a powerful USP that will attract customers for years to come. I'll start with three secrets that will practically force your customers to do business with you instead of your competition. These are conceptual items that, if you'll keep them in mind as you develop your USP, will help you fashion one that does the job in a potent and consistent manner.

Number One: The More Unique You Are, The Better

There's a reason it's called a *Unique* Selling Position. At its root, a USP is really just what that separates you from your competition, whether that's one thing or several; it's what makes a person choose to do business with you rather than the guy down the street. That means you have to think about what makes you different from the next guy selling the same thing.

Let's say you sell a certain type of widget, and there are hundreds of people in your market selling that widget. There are still ways you can set yourself apart from your competitors. Thus could be anything from a catchy name or slogan, to how fast you ship your product. Maybe everyone else takes four to five days to ship the widget — but you do it in 24 hours. These are just a few off-the-cuff examples: there are all kinds of things you can come up with if you put a little skull-sweat into it. **Your USP can even be so unique that it's controversial. That makes it newsworthy.**

That, in turn, leads to free publicity. If you have the right USP in place, it's going to give you a competitive advantage, because you're the company the media is focusing on — and as a result, you're the business that your target market is going to focus on.

Here's a related point. **As much as you want to attract the right people to your business, it's equally as important to repel the *wrong* people.** What that means is, you've got to have enough courage to not worry about ticking off the wrong people. You're looking for just one type of person; that's all you care about, and that's who your message is aimed at. The more controversial it is, assuming that you don't repel the kind of people that you're looking for, the better. Many businesses, I think, are preoccupied with trying to be lukewarm. They're trying to attract everybody, and their messages have no real power to their potential customers whatsoever. It's like jumping up and down in the ocean instead of in a puddle.

Number Two: Know Your Competitors Better Than They Know Themselves

You can't assume that just because you sell the same widget as your competitors, you understand how those competitors operate. Take Sam Walton, the founder of Wal-Mart; he knew better. When he was starting out, he spent more time in K-Mart than most K-Mart managers! He knew that the best way to make Wal-Mart successful was to know the competition extremely well — to know it inside and out. He spent months learning how they did business, what their prices were, and the products they sold — and in the process, he got kicked out of several K-Marts. Obviously, that didn't stop him.

If you have a physical storefront, you need to visit other stores selling the same types of products to the same types of customers, or at least stores selling related products. You need to spend time in the store of anyone you consider a direct competitor. Talk to their employees: if you can do it and they don't know who you are, that's great. But if they're smart and they're running their business right, they know who you are — so you might have to send someone else in to do some covert operations for you. If you're an Internet business and don't have a physical storefront, you can do this online as well; and it may even be easier, because to a large extent, it's anonymous. Spend plenty of time looking at other websites that sell the same kinds of products to the same types of customers. Spend some time on Google or Yahoo doing research. Search for the kinds of products you think your customers will be searching for when they find your website. If you're using Pay Per Click advertising on the search engine, spend lots of time searching the same phrases that you're advertising, in order to see what other people who are running the same keywords are advertising.

Knowing your competition, however you do it, is the best market research you'll ever do, and probably the least expensive, so it gives you the best return on your investment. Look at their literature, look at their processes, know what they're doing so you can do it better and faster and easier for the consumer. That's inexpensive education that can give you an unfair advantage over the competition. Shopping with them can also help you — so go ahead, order one of their products. How fast do you get it? What's in the package when you get it? What are they offering as an upsell or a back-end? How do they handle customer service complaints? How do they handle returns? You can get a wealth of information about your competition simply by ordering one of their products, or making a phone call inquiring about it.

Number Three: Be Specific About the Benefits You Offer

Generally speaking, being general is generally not a good way, in general, to come up with a USP. Did you get that? Obviously, I threw "general" in there several times to make the point that your USP can't be generic. *It's got to be specific.* **The reason a good USP works is because it makes your customer choose to do business with you over your competitors.** It makes

The E-Factors that influence every sale:

- Pride — Desire to be better than others...

- POWER

- Love

- Fear

- Greed

- Guilt

That's it!

These are the 5 reasons people buy anything and everything! Every reason to buy can be linked back to these 5 powerful emotional factors.

people want to seek you out. A broad USP can't do this: it doesn't provide enough punch to get your customer to do business with you.

Look at Domino's Pizza, which had the best USP ever until the law made them change it: "Fresh, Hot Pizza Delivered In 30 Minutes Or Less. Guaranteed." That USP contained four elements:

- It 's fresh. (A lot of pizza isn't; it's anything but fresh.)

- It's hot.

- It's delivered within 30 minutes.

- That's guaranteed, or it's free.

It doesn't say the pizza tastes good, by the way. I think that's important. However, this simple statement is very clear, very compelling, and leaves nothing to the imagination. It delivered a specific benefit that used to separate Domino's from all the other pizza joints.

Be forewarned, however, that with specificity comes a built-in problem. **Your USP can come back to haunt you if you aren't careful, when you construct it, to make certain that you're able to deliver on your promises.** If you advertise the "fastest delivery in town" and your delivery is slow, that works against you. People who never paid attention to the speed of your delivery before will notice it now, and then they won't trust you. If you make a promise, make certain it's a promise your business can support; otherwise, you're better not to mention it at all. Too many companies, in presenting their USP, will add features that sound good but that they're not capable of delivering. That doesn't advance your business at all: in fact, it's just the reverse. It's suicide.

Let's look at Domino's again. If they hadn't been able to deliver pizza in 30 minutes, you would have been unhappy. But if you'd called a regular pizza delivery shop and it took 45 minutes or an hour to get there, you would have been perfectly satisfied, because that was normal service. Once you make a promise and it raises that expectation, failure to deliver puts you in an unfavorable light. So you have to make certain that your USP is understood clearly in its statement, that you can deliver on that USP, and more importantly, that everyone working for you knows that it's a statement you're making publicly, and that they're expected to comply with it. That's your responsibility as a business owner. If you're writing the ads, running the business, and responsible for the cash flow, you've got to make sure that your employees are in tune with your marketing message.

Refine Your USP

Here's something I want to reiterate. Your USP, whatever you come up with, isn't set in stone. **The right USP might not even come immediately; and even if it does, it may take some tinkering to get it just right.** Here's an interesting story that makes that point, one that my good friend Don Bice heard from the original Advertising Manager for Federal Express. Their classic tagline, "When it absolutely, positively has to get there overnight," took them a while to come up with — but it's made them tons of money. Here's what happened: they'd been having meeting after meeting, trying to work out a good USP, and the early efforts weren't working at all. It seems their Shipping Manager happened to be dropping some things off at one meeting, so they turned to him and said, "We're struggling with how to position our service and sell it to people." He said, "Oh, that's easy! You use us when it absolutely, positively has to get there overnight." And they said, "That's it!"

You never know where that inspiration will come from. Sometimes it comes right from your customers. **One of the secrets to developing great USPs is to hone in on the problems your customers are having, and some of the challenges they face on a daily basis.** All this is work; there's no question about it. It really does take a lot of time and effort, and it's probably not going to come overnight. But once you find that competitive advantage, you can build your entire marketing effort around it.

C'mon, Everybody Does It

An easy way to come up with your own USP is to look closely at your own company. It's funny, **but you can actually create a USP not by doing something differently than all your competitors, but by advertising things that *everybody* does in the marketplace but that your customers don't know about.** For example, let's say you do something behind the scenes that your customers never know about, and let's say everyone else in the same marketplace does the exact same thing. You can stand up and say, "Look, this is how we do it. This is the care that we take. This is how we process orders. This is how we handle *your* order." Just by bringing that to the forefront, all of a sudden you've got a USP. Any of your competitors can say, "We do that too!" But if they do, all of a sudden they become the "me too" person, following *you*.

Here's an excellent story of how this works. In 1919 Claude Hopkins, a famous copywriter and marketing expert, was hired by Schlitz Beer. At the time, Schlitz was in something like tenth or fifteenth place in beer sales. They were desperate to boost their sales, so they hired Hopkins. He went in and asked all sorts of questions about what they did in their business, so they walked him through the factory and showed him the brewing process. He was shown how they washed the beer bottles repeatedly, how carefully they chose the yeast, and all the copper kettles and other equipment they used. He was absolutely fascinated by the entire process, so he went to the people at Schlitz and said, "Look, why aren't you telling people about this? This is absolutely amazing! People would love this!" The Schlitz people replied, "But everybody else does the exact same thing." And Claude Hopkins pointed out, "Yes, but nobody *knows* that. If you use your marketing to tell everyone how you brew your beer, it'll put you above and beyond everybody else. You'll be the first in this category, even though your competitors do these things too."

The Schlitz people did what Hopkins told them. They told people how beer was made, and in six months' time Schlitz was the best-selling beer in America. Did they have to change anything they did? No; **all they did was tell their customers about something they were already doing for them. They made the product interesting. It's a common product in a very competitive market, but they got around that by telling people what most brewers would assume everybody already knew. They brought it to the forefront, and that became their USP.** You see, sometimes you've got to educate your customers. You have to teach them what makes you special; don't just take it for granted. Then dramatize those facts to make them appealing to people so that it really *does* interest them, and they'll appreciate that.

That's why when you're doing your research, you should think about whatever it is you're already doing just like everybody else, but that maybe nobody knows about. If you tell your customers about it, it sounds like inside information, or a revelation, or something new and different, maybe even a breakthrough — *even if everybody else in your field is doing it.*

You're Selling What Now?

Here's something that many people never even consider when

developing their USP. Obviously you're selling a product or a service, and you know what that is. But here's how it fits into crafting a USP. You have to ask yourself, "What am I *really* selling?

A perfect example is a company I know of that markets an office prospecting system. This is a management and organization service that shows you how to prospect for new clients, how to handle the clients once they're in your system, and how to get all the employees on the same page as to how this all works. That was how they marketed the product at first, plain and simple. Then at some point they asked themselves, "What are we *really* selling?"

Here's the USP they came up with. The headline for their ad was, "It puts your office on autopilot so you can spend the afternoon playing golf." Why would they do such a thing? Because they took time to back away and take a good look at their market. They asked themselves, "Who's most likely to give us money for what we're offering?" They discovered that many of the people who use this kind of system are golfers, who are looking for any excuse to get out of the office, hold all their messages, and get out on the golf course. When they realized this, they crafted their USP to target those people, and they recreated their product. In other words, they're no longer selling this unique system with all the software that does this and that and has all these wonderful features. They're selling golf time. Their whole selling point is that it frees you up and puts everything on autopilot so you can go play golf. It's a great example of how you should deconstruct what your service or product is and ask yourself, what are you *really* selling?

A Few Other Options to Consider

I think making things risk-free can be a great USP. For example, a company called Investment Rarities in Minnesota offers a two-year, money-back guarantee when you buy gold bouillon or gold coins from them — which is ideal if the market takes a downturn. Seaside Buick in San Diego offers another great example. When you buy a car from most dealers, you lose thousands of the dollars the instant you drive it off the lot — but what Seaside Buick does is offer a five-day money-back guarantee. For most products and services, five days doesn't count for much; but when you're buying a new car, it counts big-time! You take the car, you drive it anywhere you want for five days, and if you didn't like something about it, you can bring it back and get your money back in full.

My company, M.O.R.E., Inc., produces information products. In our marketplace, which is loaded with skepticism, one of the USPs we used for years was a lifetime money-back guarantee, until our lawyer made us change it — he told us it wasn't legal. For years, that was the deal our company offered: if you weren't happy with the product anytime within your lifetime or ours, you could get your money back — no questions asked. It blew the customers away, because they were used to dealing with lots of hassles with other companies whenever they tried to get their money back, even after 10 or 20 days, let alone years after they made the purchase!

Offering special incentives is another great way to refine your USP. Give people something extra. This works especially well if your competitors are selling the exact same products as you. Another good USP is to zero in on the needs of your market. If you're a sporting goods store, tell your customers that you have all the products they need for fishing, hunting, golf, or archery, or that you specialize in serving people with special health needs.

Here's another thing to keep in mind: try to get your USP in everything that describes what you do. For example, you can clearly telegraph a benefit, or at least what it is that you're selling, through the name on your business cards. When somebody asks you what do you do, describe what you do. Turn *that* into a USP. Don't just say, "I provide financial services," if that's what it might be. **Figure out what you're really selling, find the benefits that you can telegraph to that customer or prospect, and use that to describe what you do. You don't need to use catchy, cute, clever phrases in your USP or business name — everybody else does that.**

Instead of playing around with words, create a name for your business that telegraphs the major benefit of what you're offering, so people don't have to scratch their heads and wonder. Make it so that when they see you listed in the Yellow Pages, they can determine, just from the title of your business, exactly what it is that you're offering. If you're creating products, make sure that the product name telegraphs your USP and makes that benefit clear. Promotions work the same way. If you want to name the promotion, try to integrate your USP into the name of that promotion so people don't have to figure it out on their own. I'm not trying to say that your customers are stupid, but they'll appreciate it if you make life a little bit easier for them.

It's easy to get caught up in being the business owner and to forget what it's like to be the customer. What you need to do is take off the business-owner hat for just a moment, put on a consumer's hat, and pretend you've got a problem your customer wants solved. Write down the things people might be looking for. What's their exact problem? What's the exact end result they want? What do they have going on in their minds when they're looking for the product or service you're providing? In doing that, you're going to achieve some insight you didn't have before.

If you're so close to the business that you can't do this yourself, it wouldn't hurt to talk to some of your consumers; or you might be able to talk to some friends who've used your product and services. You have to get into that customer's mindset; don't keep working from your own mindset, saying to yourself, "Well, they *should* want this," and, "They *should* want that," and, "They *should* be interested in this." What they *should* want doesn't matter. It's what they *do* want that actually matters. Once you find out what they *do* want, you can build your USP around that.

Cop a Realistic Attitude About Your USP

Remember this painful fact: not everyone is as enamored with your business as you are. You may love your company and your products, but you also have to realize that we live in a busy culture that's saturated with marketing. People are busy; they've got their heads full of all kinds of different things, and the bottom line is this: most people just don't give a damn about your business. That's the one thing a lot of businesspeople never stop to consider, and sure, it's understandable. Our companies are our livelihoods; they're extensions of ourselves. We love what we do, and so naturally we suffer from the delusion of thinking that other people give a damn — but they really don't. I hate to break it to you, but sometimes even our own families and friends don't really give a damn about our businesses.

Many entrepreneurs make the mistake of thinking that people care about their product or service, or that all they have to do is put an ad in the Yellow Pages and say that they're in business at a certain location, and the people will come. But remember, this is exactly what a good USP isn't. Most people won't spare something like this a second glance. It's not necessarily that they're lazy and apathetic; in most cases, they're just plain busy. On top of that, they're so bombarded with marketing that they usually don't have the time to think about or care about what

Work on your business — not in it. Be the architect of your business — not the worker or foreman.

Definition: The architect designs the building — and sees to it that his plans are followed by the builders.

The same is true in business. We must design successful marketing systems — and then monitor them closely.

Work ON it — not IN it.

they're hearing. If anything, they feel like they're overwhelmed with advertising messages.

If you can realize that most people not only don't give a damn about your advertising, your company, and what you're trying to sell them, but on the contrary, actually hate it — then you're of the proper mindset. Once you realize how fed up with advertising people are, you can start adjusting your message so it really does do all the great things I'm talking about here. Whatever it is you're selling, you have to get people to stop and pay attention — and that's what a USP is all about. If you can't get them to pay attention to you, they've got plenty of other things to do to keep themselves occupied.

Avoid Change for Change's Sake

If a USP just isn't working for you, don't hesitate to change it — but beware of changing a successful USP just because you've grown bored with it. This happens far more often than it should: marketing people get tired of the same old advertising, even though it works. **Somebody goes through a tremendous amount of time, money, and effort to develop a USP, to put together some great marketing campaigns, business just grows by leaps and bounds, and then they get bored and start changing everything.**

A good example is the Schlitz story I mentioned earlier. Several years after Hopkin's innovative idea, some not-so-bright marketer said, "You know, we need a catchphrase for our Schlitz Beer," and they changed the whole marketing strategy to this: "Schlitz, the beer that made Milwaukee famous." And now Schlitz Beer is nowhere in the Top 10, or even Top 20, of all beer sold in America. In fact, the company barely exists as such, these days. This shows you how you can have the right USP, and how you can go back and change it and get the wrong one.

In advertising they have a saying: "By the time the client gets bored with the message and wants to change, it's probably making its first impression on the public." Here's a word to the wise: **get a good thing going and keep it going. A great way to think of your marketing is to picture it as a parade. Your business is on a parade float, and at the beginning you're all excited about being on the float and you see the flowers, and the papier-mâché, and you're waving at the people and having a good time. Then, after about 30 minutes you're getting hot, and you realize that the** papier-mâché is flaking off, and you're sweating and you hate it, and you want to jump off that float and get onto another. What you don't realize is that the people the parade is passing by are seeing you for the first time. They're excited. They're waving. Down the way a bit, there are even more people who've never seen you before, and they're excited to see you. Further on down, there are even more people happy to see you!

The long and the short of it is, most companies just get bored, because they see the same marketing every day. They want to jump off that float, even though it's still effective. "Oh, that slogan is so old. These sales letters are bad. Our USP is worn out; we've had it now for six months." So what? Some companies keep the same USP for years and years. Why would they do that? Because it continues to work. Don't change your USP just because you're bored. If it's working, if it's making money — stick to it.

In business, we tend to monkey with things more than we

should, when if we'd let the customers continue to tell us what they want by studying their buying patterns, we'd be a lot better off. If the USP stops working because sales are low, then by all means change it; find a new USP, adjust it, tweak it, do whatever you need to. But to change your USP just because you're tired of it or bored with it is a bad idea. If the customers still like it and your sales are good, keep riding that baby as long as you can!

Summing It Up

As I wind down this chapter, I want to give you a quick recap of the things I've talked about here. **In a way, these concepts are entirely unfair to your competitors — because if you use them to create your USP, they'll separate you from every other competitor in your marketplace and let you dominate that marketplace.** But hey — there's a reason this is called the Ruthless Marketing System, right? You've got to be ruthless if you want to stay alive in our increasingly competitive marketplace.

Identify the Enemy

Take a look at the people who sell the exact same goods and services in your marketplace. **Who are your top five competitors, and why?** You've got to figure out what they're doing right, what they're doing wrong. What do they do to attract and retain the best customers and clients? You've got to spy on them, study them, become a customer. You've got to know them better than they know themselves. You've got to know their strengths and weaknesses and try to focus in on those, because nobody makes money by accident. If they're doing well consistently, they're doing something right.

Identify the Biggest Problems and Unfulfilled Needs in Your Market

What are the three biggest problems your prospects and customers face on a daily basis? **What do your best prospects**

and customers want and need that they're not getting anywhere else? Answer these questions right, and you'll have a great USP. Build your Claims Matrix, so you can find where the gaps are. Where are the unfulfilled promises? Where are the biggest dissatisfactions? Work to create the great solutions to the biggest problems. To do this, you've got to brainstorm, brainstorm, and brainstorm!

Make Your Benefits Clear To Your Customers

Every USP requires a clear statement of benefits. Don't assume that your customers know what they'll get when they deal with you instead of Joe Blow down the street. Tell them exactly what you can do for them, and why they should come to you instead. If you've got the best-quality muffins in town, flaunt it. If your service is unique, take advantage of that. People need to know how you're going to make their lives better.

Just Get Your USP Out There

I can't overstate the importance of formulating your USP and getting it out there where your clients can see it. It's too easy to get caught in the paralysis of analysis. You say to yourself, "It has to be perfect! I've got to get it just right!" Well, no, it doesn't. As I've made clear, you can refine your USP after you've launched it, as long as you don't overdo it. Don't think your USP has to be perfect right out of the box. As a small businessperson, you have the ability to be flexible. **If you can come up a great USP right now, and if down the road there's an ever better one and an even better advantage to your business, then you can change it.** Take a little bit of time and effort, get your USP out there and, believe me, even if it's not the best of the best of the best, you're going to be head and shoulders above the rest of your competitors.

Refine That USP

This one goes hand-in-glove with the previous point. Once

MARKETING SECRET #7

The universal common denominator of why people buy:

People buy things to feel better about themselves!

- Everyone wants to feel better about themselves.

- The products/ services they buy let them do it somehow/somewoay. (emotional)

your USP's out there, you can refine it as needed. Here are some good guidelines to follow: keep it short and clear. Keep it benefit-oriented. Make your claims believable. Make them measurable, if possible, as in time or quantity. Avoid defining your USP on price alone; someone can always beat you on that. Make your claim unique, and use your proposition everywhere you can.

That's a good place to end this chapter. I hope you understand a little better the fact that putting together a decent USP and making money with it really does take an intimate understanding of your best customers, their likes and dislikes, the challenges they face, the problems that keep them up at night, and the frustrations that they live with. The more you know about all of that, plus the more aware you are of those few competitors who are out there kicking butt in the marketplace, the better. Watch them closely. **Good companies are few and far between; that makes them easy to spot, if you know what to look for.** Keep a close eye on them, and you'll find the right type of messages, through experimentation, because your customers will respond. They'll respond with their checkbooks, their credit cards, and their cash.

Direct-Response Marketing

In this chapter, I'll introduce you to Direct-Response Marketing, and show you how you can use this powerful tool to dramatically increase your profits. The tips, tricks. and strategies I'll reveal to you here can make you huge sums of money, but you're going to have to read this chapter several times to really understand it. **Direct-Response Marketing is a complicated subject that deserves in-depth study.**

At its most basic, Direct-Response Marketing is whatever you do to get your customers to respond to you directly. It's not the kind of brand awareness you see when Pepsi or AT&T run a commercial on TV. That's not really asking you to do anything; it's just them getting their name out there. Direct-Response Marketing, on the other hand, is meant to get people to respond to you directly: to pick up the phone and call you, or to fill out an order form and fax it or mail it to you. **It's anything you do in business to get people to order from you, or to request more information, or to take a specific action.**

In some ways, I consider Direct-Response Marketing an art form. It's the process of identifying the audience most likely to purchase your product or service, and then approaching them directly at the right time to solicit their business, using a direct-to-consumer advertising medium. This can be postcards or other mailings, sales calls, special emails, handing out discount cards — **any form of advertising that directly targets potential and existing customers,** rather than something just thrown out there in hopes that someone will remember you when it comes time to fix the muffler or buy roses for Mother's Day. I call it an art form because it takes a while to understand and perfect the strategies you *must* use to truly match the right people with the right message at the right time.

But Direct-Response Marketing is also very much a science. It's an organized, multi-step system for selling, which starts off by targeting and contacting the people who might be interested in what you're selling, in such a way that you get them to respond and make their interest clear. Then the system kicks in, working to elicit their response again and get them more involved in what it is you're offering. This works whether you do it through direct mail, on the Internet, in seminars, or even one-on-one. **The science is also in the mechanics that make it all work: the ability to put together a database, to build a list, and to market to various elements of that list.** Regardless of the advertising media or strategies you choose, you have to immerse yourself in the science if you want to even get close to achieving art.

You have to employ the mechanics of Direct-Response Marketing in a way that makes sense to **the people you want to build relationships with**. You have to get their attention, you have to grab their interest, you have to create desire, and then you have to get them to take action. If you do that right, eventually you'll be able to create your masterpiece — the kind of life you want to live, lubricated by copious amounts of money.

The Name of the Game

Your goal with Direct-Response Marketing is to get an immediate action from your prospect, whether it's a visit to your business, a call, an order, a purchase, a request for more information, or a promise. To accomplish any of these things, you need to create **salesmanship in print**. Not only does your Direct-Response Marketing strategy need to evoke an immediate action, but it also has to do everything a real salesman would do, in terms of generating that response. **Just like a living, breathing**

salesman, here's what that a good Direct-Response Marketing campaign does:

- It tells the prospect about the benefits of the product;

- It overcomes objection;

- It answers questions;

- It provides a guarantee; and

- It makes promises.

A good Direct-Response Marketing campaign does all these things and more; it has to, in order to succeed. I think the biggest benefit of Direct-Response Marketing over face-to-face salesmanship or even telemarketing is that you have the power to let Yellow Page ads, sales letters, classified ads, or display ads in the newspaper, magazines or on the Internet generate the response you're looking for. Direct-Response Marketing allows you to multiply your effort, to reach a lot more people, and generate a lot more responses without wasting your time — and that makes it a very powerful strategy indeed.

In order to work effectively, Direct-Response Marketing has to be a very targeted form of marketing. Think of a rifle, versus a shotgun. With Direct-Response Marketing, you don't just blast out a message to everyone at random: **your message is delivered in the clearest and most compelling way possible, to the specific people who are most likely to buy and then continue to buy from you.** Those people could be highly qualified prospects that you've identify through various methods, or they can be established customers, people with whom you already have an ongoing relationship.

Marketers use lots of metaphors to describe Direct-Response Marketing. In addition to being a combination of art and science, to many of us it's also a combination of sport and war. This is a

Strong motivators...

- Some products/services can be sold because people want to avoid a negative situation

- People will do more to avoid pain — than to gain pleasure

- Use the P.A.S. (Problem — Agitate — Solution) Formula

fun way of making money. You can be very strategic using this marketing method, just as a couple of generals would be when planning how to stage an attack on their enemy. Because make no mistake: no matter how much you'd like to believe otherwise, **your direct competitors are your enemies**. They're out there trying to get the same dollars you're trying to get, and you can't let that happen.

Laying a Firm Foundation

Direct Marketing is a system for selling, and if **you don't have a system for selling, then you're at the mercy of your customer's system for buying — and they don't have one.** What most businesses do — sadly for them, but fortunately for you — is the direct opposite of Direct-Response Marketing. They set up shop, put up some signs, and maybe run the occasional radio ad or newspaper spot, but they do it in such a way that it's mildly effective at best. They're not using Direct-Response Marketing to get people into their selling system.

Now, in order to do Direct-Response Marketing right, you need to start with a firm foundation. One excellent way to do this is to achieve an intimate understanding of what I call the *Three Keys to Effective Direct-Response Marketing*. These keys will help you do Direct-Response

Marketing right; I've seen a lot of people make a lot of mistakes that could easily have been avoided if they'd just done the simple things I'm going to tell you to do here. The Three Keys are relatively straightforward, and they strip Direct-Response Marketing down to its basic elements. Without further ado, here's what you have to have to do effective Direct-Response Marketing:

- The right message

- The right audience

- The right time

Or to put it all together into one sentence, you've got to **carry the right message to the right audience at the right time.** I consider this the Golden Rule of Direct-Response Marketing.

Many marketers boil this concept down to what they call the KISS Principle, where KISS stands for "Keep It Simple, Stupid." I think that's a little offensive, so I'll use my own term, thank you. Now, if you don't get the right message to the right audience at the right time, you're going to hear "no" a lot more than you'll hear "yes." **Instead of using a shotgun, pull up that high-powered rifle**, identify exactly who the prospect is who's most likely to buy your product, and go directly to that consumer using a direct-to-consumer advertising medium. In the following sections, I'm going to discuss all these things in greater detail, and in the order I think is most important.

Key One: The Audience

If you don't play to the right audience, you're never going to have a very good response to anything you do. You've failed right from the beginning: game over, time to go home. Identifying the right people is the most important key to successful Direct-Response Marketing, and I suggest you use three methods to accomplish this.

First is what I call "customer hijacking" — or **letting your competition do your work for you.** This is simply where you go out and rent a list of your competition's customers and then try to make them your own. It's not possible for every industry, but it's the number one tactic I suggest *if* it's possible. So if you're Sears, and J. C. Penney is selling appliances, you try to get a list of those people they've recently sold appliances to. Then you can send them a Direct Mail piece that gives them the option of buying their next appliance from you.

Second is demographic profiling: analyzing your target audience and **coming up with the profile of your ultimate customer or target audience.** In using demographics like age, gender, income level, and location, you're basically looking for anything that helps you identify who's most likely to buy your products and services. Once you've figured that out, you can go out and acquire a list of clients who meet those criteria. You're going to use list brokers for both customer hijacking and demographic profiling.

Third is customer corralling. This is where you capture information on your past or current customers, and add them to a list so you can continue to solicit business. Keep in mind that **the easiest sale you're ever going to make is to a customer to whom you've already sold.** A good example of this is Harrah Casinos' Loyalty Programs. You go in there to gamble one time, they get you on a little card, and pretty soon you're getting more mail than you've ever known — and you're going back to Harrah's a lot more often.

Key Two: Your Message

Now, let's talk about the right message. You need to **study your products or services from your customer's perspective.** Remember, it's all about them; you have to keep in mind their view, which can be summarized as WIIFM — *What's In It For Me?* That's what your prospects want to know. So build your message around the strongest benefits to your customer, and keep in mind that there are only five real reasons people buy anything: greed, guilt, fear, pride, or love. We marketers call this the *psychographic* of your audience, as opposed to the demographic; and **the two most important of those psychographic motives are greed and fear.** That's why you see so many commercials that play on people's greed, or that make them afraid that they're doing something wrong: raising their children wrong, not brushing their teeth enough, or not wearing the right deodorant.

You need to **understand the emotional reasons that people buy products and services. Make sure you build your benefits toward one or more of those reasons.** Identify your customer's strongest motives to buy, and you're going to do very well identifying the right message.

Key Three: the Right Time

Once you've identified the right audience and the right message, you need to identify the time your prospects are most likely to purchase your product or service. For example, if you run a mortgage company, aim your message at people who are selling their houses. If a person's selling a house, they'll most likely need to buy a new house shortly thereafter — so if you hit them with a mortgage opportunity right then and there, there's a good chance they'll take it. If you wait three weeks or a month after your prospect puts his property on the market, chances are that he's already found another mortgage if he was planning to buy another piece of property. Therefore, you need to respond within a few days, no more. If you plan this properly and do it correctly, the time *will* be right.

Effective Direct-Response Marketing is all about the right audience, the right message, and the right timing. And while I've discussed Direct-Response Marketing as an art form, don't worry about going out there and trying to paint the *Mona Lisa* right off the bat. **It's kind of like playing chess. You might start out a bit** slow, but you're going to get better at it the more you do it. Like chess, Direct-Response Marketing takes a day to learn and a lifetime to master; but use these guidelines, and you'll have a solid foundation to build your business on.

What Kind of Bait's on Your Hook?

One thing you should be aware of from the get-go is that **Direct-Response Marketing isn't cheap.** If you use it right you can make millions, but as the old saying goes, it takes money to make money. Continuing with the mortgage example, here's an interesting way that some people have attracted new customers. They combine the right message with the right audience at the right time, they send their message by Federal Express — already an expensive proposition — and then they sweeten the proposition by throwing a $100 bill in that Federal Express package. That's right — a $100 bill. You see, they know it's a numbers game, but it's also a game of finding the right people to deliver your message to, and knowing that **you can spend a lot more money to reach that right person** (assuming that other things — your price points and your profit margins — are high).

So these marketers are throwing a $100 bill in a Federal Express envelope, and then sending a personalized letter along with it. There's none of that "Dear Friend" crap — that's counterproductive. Instead, they're saying, "Dear John: Why have I sent you a $100 bill by Federal Express? Two reasons: 1) Your time is very valuable, so I'm paying you well to spend a good, solid hour looking over everything in this package; and 2) I believe you're the type of person I'm looking for, and I'm willing to back up my beliefs with a solid investment." That's an excellent example of getting the right message to the right prospect at the right time, and not being afraid to spend a lot of money in the process.

So many people fail with Direct-Response Marketing, and they don't have to. This is a $300 billion a year industry; so why doesn't it work for them? When you dig a little deeper, it turns out that **they didn't have their hearts in it**. They sent out some postcards, they didn't get the results they expected, and they gave up. They thought they were doing Direct-Response Marketing — but they're really weren't. *You have to spend money with Direct-Response Marketing to make money.* It could be worth it to send out $100 bills once you know what your customers are worth. You want to get their attention, and their time is valuable, and paying them for it is a great way to grab them by the throat and make them give you a fair hearing.

P. T. Barnum, who is one of my heroes — a great, great marketer — once said, "Don't try to catch a whale by using a minnow as bait. **"If there's one general mistake I see a lot, one that people who are brand new to Direct-Response Marketing are making over and over, it's that they want huge results from the very beginning.** They're expecting enormous things from this form of marketing, which it can and does deliver to the people who understand how to use it. But they're starting out trying to capture a whale by using a minnow as bait, and in doing so they're being *far* too conservative. **As long as you've found the right customer and the right message, and the rest of your mechanics are in place, you can afford to spend a ton of money to reach that person."**

If I said this approach always works, I'd be lying. You don't know for sure what's going to happen. Even if it's the right thing to do, you're going to reach a certain percentage of people who can't follow through because other things are going on in their lives. Maybe, for example, they've just broken their leg, or they're getting a divorce, or they've lost their job. So you won't catch every prospect, but remember: you won't catch any if you use the wrong bait. Don't be afraid to gamble a little, because if you're trying to catch a whale by using a minnow as bait, you'll never have any real success.

Knowing What You're Doing

Here's another thing I'd like to add about the person who says, "Well, I sent out a postcard one time and I didn't get any responses." When I hear that, I say, "Let me see your sales material." Usually, I find that they've done a terrible job of getting their message across. Sometimes people believe they're great writers, and they're not; or they're not focusing on right kind of communication. They may write copy that sounds really good and has a lot of big words in it, and what those big words do to a lot of people is turn them off. Many of their readers might not understand them, and **a confused mind says "no" automatically.** Also, if a prospect doesn't understand a word, they may subconsciously feel like they're stupid. They shut off at that point.

There are all kinds of factors that go into Direct-Response Marketing that a novice isn't even aware of. They may have written a postcard, and had their buddy with an English degree edit it so it's grammatically correct and looks nice, but it just doesn't elicit the response they wanted — because they didn't really know what they wanted it to do, or they didn't know how to compel people to say "yes." **In order to solicit business, you need to get into those psychographic factors I mentioned before (fear, greed, guilt, love, and pride), as well as the nuts-and-bolts science of what makes people say yes.**

If you don't know how to do this, don't try to wing it: either hire people who do, or go find people who've done it and emulate them. Don't steal from them, but model your copy after what they've done. **Do the things you know have already been successful for others, then fine-tune those strategies so they can work for you.** There are a lot of strategies floating around out there, and lots of little ways to tweak your performance. Even the colors of your postcards can make a difference in response. As a Direct Response Marketer, you're going to have to do a lot of things you've never done before. Think of all these things as broadening your education.

You'll want to continue to market to your prospects in a systemized manner, using follow-up campaign sequences — one following the other. This will cost you some money, but it's justified. Once you implement the three keys I talked about earlier — getting the right message to the right people at the right time — you're not done. That's really where you start. Do those things right, and you're going to grab a nice percentage of your target audience; they'll go through your selling process, and you'll make some money. But you need to continue to market to them! Once you've gotten the responses from a mailing, do a second mailing, and then another. **The great thing about Direct-Response Marketing is that you know the results very quickly** — with direct mail, for example, it may take a couple of weeks, at most. Online it's even faster.

Once again, remember this: your offer does need to be tweaked and made more efficient, but it doesn't have to be a masterpiece from the word go; it just has to be good enough. Once you've got everything together and you've followed all the steps, go for it. Send it out, and learn from what happens. You don't have to flood the market right away, either — you can test and improve on your message quickly if you **start out slowly**. Start mailing, testing, sending out little bits and pieces, and see what happens.

AIDA Ain't Just an Opera

Here's an interesting acronym that some of my fellow marketers find useful: AIDA. It stands for:

- **A**ttention

- **I**nterest

- **D**esire

- **A**ction

AIDA dovetails nicely with the three keys we've already discussed here. But these four elements have more to do with the overall process once you've already targeted your prospects and figured out what you want to say, and you know you have the timing down.

Once you've done all these things, look at the actual Direct Marketing media available: the piece, the letter, the ad, the email message, or whatever it is. **First of all, you need to grab your prospect's Attention**, and typically you're going to do that with your headline. That's what it'll be in print or on a website; if it's an email, it's your subject. If you're addressing people in a conference, it's the first thing you say. If it's a postcard, it's in bold print. The headline has to grab their attention and make them want to read further. That's its only purpose — to grab their attention, and get them interested in continuing to read.

One of the greatest headlines ever was Dale Carnegie's "How To Win Friends and Influence People." "How to" headlines are not only often the easiest to come up with — because you already have the first two words down — but quite often they're also the most effective. What should that "how to" promise? **It needs to be benefit-laden**. I've mentioned "What's In It For Me?" already. WIIFM is the essence of writing your headline.

Once you get their attention, you need to grab their Interest. Quite often, this is done with a sub-headline that states your Unique Selling Proposition. As I made clear in the last chapter, a USP is what sets you apart from everyone else. It answers the question in the prospect's mind: "Why should I deal with this person or company, or buy this service, or get involved in this, or even accept this free report over all the others out there?"

Your next goal is to stimulate a Desire as they get into your offer. Most people think in words, but they take those words and put them into pictures. A picture is a stronger, more effective way of thinking. Most people, being visual, require the painting of these word pictures in their minds, and that's what you want to do as you tell your story. You want them to be in this story; they're the star of the show you're creating here. That's how you really create desire in people: by the way you place them in the copy, and the way you overcome their initial apprehension. Testimonials from people who have benefited from what you offer can work wonders here.

Now we come to the second "A," which is Action. You have to **make sure that it's easy and convenient for prospects to become customers.** This is where you ask for their response, whether it's an order, or for them to call an 800 number, or to send an email — whatever it is you want them to do. This is where you make it convenient for them to respond. Give your prospects several ways to get in touch with you. You don't want to give them too many choices, ever, on anything, but you want to give them basic choices. This is where understanding your customer is really important. Some people may have misgivings about certain ways of responding to you, so you want to give them options that are comfortable for them. Maybe the psychodemographics of your customer base makes them more likely to pick up the phone and call a number; or maybe they'd prefer to fax their order in. You should also give them the option to mail their order in, even if you're strictly doing an online transaction. That's a big mistake I often see online: not even offering that option. The way a lot of websites work — you put your credit card in or you don't buy, and that's a mistake. Some people just don't feel safe putting their credit card number out there in cyberspace.

Calls to Action

Let's go back to something I touched on earlier: the way that **many businesses try Direct-Response Marketing, then dump it quickly because it doesn't work for them.** That's because they're not using it right. I've discussed using the right bait, and this next point plays into that concept: you have to give your customers a great offer. Some businesses try Val-Pak, where you get all these little full-color inserts about various businesses; you've probably gotten these packets yourself. But that's not Direct-Response Marketing. That's just coupon marketing. Most of the coupons are horrible because they're either designed by the advertiser, who doesn't know how to market properly, or they're designed by a person who wants to get the work done and move on to the next customer. Yes, you're sending that coupon out to a list of human beings, but it's not targeted, and the ads are uninspired. If you look at them, basically what they're saying is, "Hey, we're your plumber! We've been in business for 80 years. We're the best in the business!" That's not Direct-Response Marketing, because that doesn't evoke an action. Someone who gets that will say, "Wow, they've been in business 80 years. I'd go crazy if I had to do plumbing for 80 years! Poor suckers!" And then they throw it away.

You have to give people an offer that will evoke an action. Maybe you've done some image advertising, where you just try to get your name out in front of people, say through postcards or in the

Yellow Pages, and hope that somebody will contact you because your ad just happened to appear when they had a plumbing problem, or they needed an attorney, or whatever your business is — but that's not going to happen very often. You absolutely have to target your market, you have to get the right message to them, and you have to use the right timing. **You need to capture their attention by making them an offer that will actually get them to take an action — whether that's calling your business, coming by, or purchasing something from you.**

One great example is a gentleman by the name of Bob Stupak, the founder of the Stratosphere Casino in Las Vegas. As you know, most Las Vegas casinos do image advertising. They don't say, "Come on in, we've got this special deal for you," and things like that; instead, they've got these beautiful billboards and beautiful ads, and they show the fountains out in front and the people gambling and having fun inside. That's supposed to be enough to evoke an action in you, to have you come to their casino. Well, Bob Stupak was a great marketer as well as a great gambler. **When he started out, the Stratosphere was a tiny casino, and he needed to pull people in, so he created an offer: for $198 you got a three-day, two-night stay at his casino. You paid this in advance, before you ever showed up, and you had an entire year to use it.** He ran his ads in *Parade* magazine and did Direct Mail and got his ads out everywhere. It wasn't an image ad; it was an actual *offer*. For $198 you got a three-day, two-night stay at the casino, but you also got two tickets to their headliner show, several meal coupons, as much as $500 in slot tokens, and $200 in casino chips.

People bought into Stupak's offer like crazy. He was selling literally tens of thousands of these packages, and that's how **he built the Stratosphere into a multi-billion dollar business.** It was a hot offer, and he continued to make it better and throw in more bonuses over time. Here's the kicker: plenty of people bought the offer, but only a relatively small percentage ever actually showed up at his casino. So all those people who didn't show up, didn't take up space in the room, didn't come to get their chips — they'd still paid all that money, and he got to pocket that.

Now you're thinking, "Okay, that's a casino. How am I going to make a hot offer like that to my customers?" **Use your imagination. There are people in every business niche — plumbers, attorneys, restaurateurs — who are making hot offers people can't turn down.** There aren't very many of them, but they're out there. Here's another example: there's a certain restaurateur who realized early on that the lifetime value of each of his customers was very high. He knew that if he could get people into his restaurant to sit down and eat a meal, they'd come back not one or two times, but five times, 20 times, 100 times. They'd be coming back for many years, which made the lifetime value of the typical customer literally thousands of dollars.

So, what was his offer? He mailed out sales letters to people in his area, and offered them a free meal. That's right. I'm not talking about a "buy one, get one free" deal, or a child's meal free if you bought an adult meal. There were no strings attached: he offered an actual free meal. You got the entrée, you got an appetizer, you got your drink. Every single thing was free! In his sales letter, he told the truth about why he wanted you to come in and enjoy this free meal: it was because he knew you would come back again and again, since the food was so great. **His business practically**

exploded, because people thought that was an incredible deal. They'd come in, enjoy the meal, and then come back again and again.

This takes us back to the concept of how much money you're willing to spend to get people into your business. A lot of business people are scared to go too far out on a limb; they don't want to spend too much of their limited advertising budget. Maybe a few cents for postage on a postcard is all they think they can afford. **But if you're delivering the services people want, and you're giving great value, and you have customers with a very high lifetime value, you can afford to make great offers in order to get prospects in the door.** You can go negative on that initial offer and still make money.

Your offer doesn't even have to be a price deal. Let's say you're stuck on your price: maybe you can't give your customers the lowest price out there, or maybe you don't even want to try. Instead, give more for what you're selling. For example, let's say you're a dentist. You can offer a lot more things than just a regular cleaning. You might say, "Come in, and we're going to give you a regular cleaning and a personalized toothbrush. Then we're going to have a customer appreciation party, and every six months you can get a free ticket for yourself and your family. We've got free drinks and free food." You can throw anything in there! **There's all sorts of crazy stuff you can do to create a great offer that catches prospects and brings them in.** If you make good on your promises, you're going to keep them.

So get over your fear of trying something wild to draw your customers in. The response can be phenomenal. Make a tremendous offer; do things that shock people; do things that would scare most business owners to death. Now, you don't have to be a fool about it. **One of the greatest things about Direct-Response Marketing is that you can test all kinds of wild and crazy and outrageous ideas to a small group of customers, so you're not really risking a lot of money if it doesn't work.** You can make sure you take what we call a stratified sample of your list and market to that — assuming you've built up a list.

You can stratify or segment your list by the products and services your customers buy, or by the dollar amount they spend, or by the last time they did business with you. The reason you do this is because, first of all, you can tell everything about a person from their actions. When somebody's buying a certain type of product or service from you, that speaks volumes. Or, if you have a few customers who are spending ten times more money than the rest of your customers, those people are showing, by the money they spend, a certain level of seriousness that the rest of your customers aren't showing. **You've got to be able to segment those smaller groups of better customers or to segment for other reasons so that you can speak directly to those groups of people in a different way than you speak to the rest of your customer list.**

So don't drop a Direct Mail campaign to your entire customer list with some crazy new idea that you're not sure is going to work. You want to see how a stratified sample is going to respond before you stretch your neck out too far. **Take little pockets of customers from your customer base and use them to test your wild and crazy stuff**, so you don't end up with a fiasco where everybody wants what you're offering, and you can't supply it to them all.

This brings up another point. When you're building your offer, you can also add a line like this one: "While supplies last." This will invoke urgency in your prospects, because now they know they'll need to hurry to get all the extra things you're throwing into your offer. In addition, this covers your bases in case you get an overzealous response. Your prospects won't mind being part of a small, select group, because when you market to a stratified sample, you're actually treating those customers special. Go ahead and tell them what you're doing; they'll appreciate being treated special. And to you, they *should* be special, because by marketing to them first, you're lowering your overall risk.

It's easy to wonder why more people don't try test-marketing offers the way I've outlined above. I think one of the big reasons they don't do it is that they don't know *how* to do it. **Most people learn marketing by looking at other marketers in their field**. So if their major competitor is running a half-page Yellow Pages ad, they think they'd better do that — instead of thinking, "Okay, maybe this isn't the right way to do it." Well, sometimes in marketing **you have to go against the flow, and do something that makes you stand head and shoulders above the crowd**. Then, once you know that, you have to get past the fear. If you own a restaurant, you may be thinking: "Good Lord, I can't even imagine giving away a free meal. I've got staff, I've got food costs, and I've got overhead. I can't even imagine making that type of a deal." You've got to break through that fear barrier.

So once you've got your offer, **test it to a small portion of your list, and see what happens.** You don't have to mail it out to 20,000 people in your area; you can mail it out to a couple of hundred people and see what the response is. If it does well, roll it out to more people. **If it doesn't do well, try something else.** It's important to at least make that offer. Because if you don't, you're going to continue to market like everybody else and continue to get the same type of response as everybody else — and in most cases, that's a pretty poor response.

If you don't already have a list, you need to build one. A lot of businesses are of the opinion that they don't need one: "I don't have a list. People come in, they buy, they leave." But not creating a list that they can use for Direct-Response Marketing is where a lot of people stumble. **There's gold in your customer list, because you're able to go back to those people, make more offers, and get them back into your business — as opposed to always going out and trying to bring brand new people in, hoping that the people who did business with you one time will remember you the second time.** If you're hoping, instead of actually mailing to a list that you've created, you're not going to be making as much money as if you were smart enough to get some simple database software, ask people for their names and contact information, and actually mail to the resulting list.

Most merchants aren't even gathering up their customers' names to begin with — and frankly, that's just ridiculous. **If you ask most business owners how much money they spend on communicating and building relationships with their existing customers, most would say, "Huh?" They may spend money to** *attract* **new customers, and they think that's what advertising and marketing is. Real marketing, however, is customer relationship marketing** — and that's now an accepted way of running a business, thanks to a lot of us Direct Response Marketers who've proven that it's successful to build and maintain those relationships. It makes sense, but so many businesses out there just don't grasp it, and they don't spend a dime to develop and maintain relationships with their customers.

Then again, **you could just do like just about everyone else, and sit around and wait for customers to come to you.** Let me share with you a story I heard from my good friend Russ von Hoelscher. He knows a guy who has a print shop in a little strip mall, and the guy's always whining and complaining about how bad business is. Russ likes the guy, but he gets sick and tired of hearing him moan. So one day Russ said, "Look, John, there's got to be 400 businesses within a five-mile radius of here. Since you've got those printing presses, why don't you just print up some sales material and I'll help you, and we can target all those businesses, and you can get them to start coming to you." And here's what the guy said to Russ: "People want printing, they can come to me." That was his whole attitude! It's ignorant, it's horrible, and it's unbelievable. Apparently, **it's easier to whine and cry and complain about how bad things are than to do a thing to change it.** Unfortunately, that mindset is more common that you might think.

It's Two, Two, *Two* Mints in One!

In the introduction to this chapter, I pointed out that Direct-Response Marketing is often considered both an art and as science, and I want to focus on that perception in this section. I want to clarify the fact that there's absolutely no way to achieve art, or even get close to it, without understanding the science involved in Direct-Response Marketing — and it's immense. So how are you going to master such a big topic, with all the variables it includes? You can start by breaking it down: learn the technology that's used to reach your market, for starters. If you're using a specific medium, you've got to understand how the process works, how to get the best rates, and what resources you have at your disposal to let you best use this medium, whether it's TV, radio, the Internet, or print. Knowing the technology used to reach your market is one key to your success, and it's all part of the science.

Another part is database management. Building or finding a list of highly qualified prospects is key. Knowing and tracking your market is also crucial. You need to know what they've purchased in the past and why they bought what they bought, because this will help you to sell them in the future.

Something I've mentioned several **times is understanding the psychological aspects of marketing — the emotional factors**

that prompt people to buy or to act. Those are, again, pride, love, fear, greed, and guilt. **Practice weaving those psycho-logical factors into your copy, into your message, into your headlines, and into your sub-headlines, because that will ultimately produce the actions you're wanting.** Now, you just can't say to yourself, "Okay, I'm going to really concentrate on pride," and whip out something that sucks in the customers. **It takes practice. It takes time to understand your style, and how you're going to invoke these factors in your audience.**

Another important factor here is communication: learning to use plain, direct, and simple words and ideas, because a confused mind says "no." If you're writing something and you think, "Man, that's really clever, the way I did that," then you might be overthinking things. There's no need to be cute with this type of writing. You want to grab them by the heart or grab them by the gonads or grab them by the mind, and the best way to do that is to do it with plain, direct speech.

Here's another big factor: **testing.** Yes, I'm repeating this too, because I want to make you see how important it is. **You don't want to commit tons of money to something you're not even the least bit sure is going to work.** Our example is the guy who tried a bunch of postcards and failed; we've talked a lot about him. He went out there, spent a lot of money on getting them printed up and on the postage to send them out — and it flopped dead. Well, that money is just gone, because he didn't test his postcard before he sent it out. He wasted his advertising dollars.

As I mentioned at the start of this section, **there's no way to achieve art without understanding the science.** It's like when you first learned to ride a bike and you had training wheels, and it was fun. You learned that you pedaled and it made you go, and you learned how the brakes worked. But then you took those training wheels off, and pretty soon you were building ramps so you could jump your bike and do crazy stunts. The same thing goes with immersing yourself in the science of Direct-Response Marketing.

You learn how it works, you learn the ins and outs and how to do it cost-effectively, and next thing you know you're jumping from ramp to ramp and you're building success on success. The art simply won't come unless you understand the science. **The science allows you to know your audience, know where to find them, know what to say, and know how to say it.**

You may never get to where Direct-Response Marketing is an art form for you, but that's a goal you can set for yourself — and maybe, someday, you'll end up painting the ceiling of the Sistine Chapel. You're always striving for that masterpiece. I've already told you that **marketing is something that takes a day to learn and a lifetime to master.** The real art comes only after a lot of work. It's no accident that the best freelance Direct Response Marketers are charging thousands of dollars for every piece they write, plus a nice chunk of the residual royalty income from the gross sales. These people have one thing in common: they've been doing it for a couple decades. There are some exceptions, but they're rare. The people in this world who are the best at this form of marketing, who really know how to do this, have been doing it for a long time.

Good Enough for Government Work

You're not going to create a perfect Direct-Response Marketing campaign from the start, but that shouldn't discourage you from trying. Remember, good enough is good enough, especially when you're starting out. You don't necessarily have to become an expert marketer before you take the plunge. The truth is, **some of the best marketing I've ever seen wasn't written by professionals — it was written by sincere business people who really love what they're doing, who really want to connect with the prospect, and who don't know all the fancy tricks and marketing secrets that somebody who's been in the business 20 years might know.** What they do have is *heart*. They have an understanding of a few of the basic principles, an understanding that you have to make an offer and you have to go to the right market with the right message at the right time. Knowing that, they're able to go out with a message that really hits home and drives business in.

Most people are convinced that advertising is best done by experts. The advertising agencies of the world want to convince you that all this is so damn complicated that you've got to be educated to do all this stuff. One of the definitions of Direct-Response Marketing I mentioned at the beginning of this chapter is that Direct-Response Marketing is salesmanship in print. I promise you, **the best salespeople aren't the ones who went to college and got a degree (with some very notable exceptions, of course). The best salespeople are the ones out there in the trenches, face-to-face, belly-to-belly, eyeball-to-eyeball with their best customers.** They've got relationships with those people. They know what those people want. They know how to give them what they want. They're out there serving them like crazy. Oftentimes the best Direct-Response Marketing doesn't look pretty; some of it really looks like crap! But it does a powerful job of getting the right message to the right customer at the right time. **It's just salesmanship: one person wanting to do business with another person.** Those are the people you want to emulate — the ones who are getting the job done, actually seeing results and generating a profit.

You're going to get better over time. Even better, once you've got it down, it's a skill you'll have forever. You're not relying on another company to create turnkey materials for you, take your money, and disappear. **You're able to create and make offers whenever you want, and that's a real power — a power to generate cash whenever you need it.** In that way, Direct-Response Marketing is the power to create money on demand. It's the opposite of just sitting around waiting for customers to come to you, which is what most people do. Good marketers are proactive: they're out there attracting people. They're not pushing; they're *pulling* people in with their messages. You can become one of those effective marketers. Once again, you don't really have to be perfect at it when you start out — it's actually quite a forgiving business. **You can make a ton of mistakes and still make a ton of money.**

Don't Overthink It

As human beings, we tend to overcomplicate things — and here's a good example. When NASA decided to send astronauts into space, on the first mission they discovered that the common ballpoint pen wouldn't work in zero gravity. So they spent millions of dollars developing a pen that would write in outer space. Now they've got one that writes underwater, upside-down, in temperatures over 100 degrees, on ice-capped mountains — in just about any condition that anyone could possibly imagine. But the Russians did something else that was pretty elegant: they used pencils instead.

There's a tendency, when you're coming up with all these ideas and strategies, to get a little overwhelmed. But **there's no need to make your marketing more complicated than it has to be. Don't try to do everything at once. You can learn one strategy and implement that strategy, then learn something else.** Look at what other people do, then tweak and fine-tune your strategy at the level you're currently at. You don't have to do everything with every promotion. There are so many different elegant, simple ways to make money in Direct-Response

Marketing.

Why Don't More People Do Direct-Response Marketing?

Most business owners don't do more Direct-Response Marketing because they don't understand it, and they don't realize it's one of the most cost-effective ways of advertising. They've been duped into thinking that other types of ads work better. Radio and television is what a lot of local businesses specifically focus their dollars on, at least in the very beginning — because it's a new business, the medium is glamorous, and they need new customers. Those media are actually training those advertisers to buy in that manner, and so advertisers often don't have the time to even consider Direct-Response Marketing.

And, of course, **there's hardly anybody showing up at their door to sell them good Direct-Response Marketing.** You've got the Yellow Page guy, who keeps bugging you to get a bigger ad. You've got the advertising specialty people, who want you to print up everything with your name on it. The newspapers and some radio and TV stations — those guys bug the hell out of you. But you don't have anybody coming along saying, "Look, I specialize in good Direct-Response Marketing that's relationship-building and long-term, using strategies that will let you quadruple your profits — or, in some cases, make more than ten of your competitors combined." There's nobody out there who's doing that as a profession.

A Dearth of Decent Offers

Here's one reason a lot of people don't do Direct-Response Marketing: they don't know how to define and create decent offers. They're simply buying the advertising they can afford, when they can afford it. Most advertisers think that Direct-Response Marketing has to be very expensive. Sure, you've got to cut through all the radio, TV, newspaper, and magazines ads, and all the crap your prospects are getting in their mail and on the Internet. Does that mean it has to cost a lot of money? No. You can give something away that has a large perceived value, but may not cost that much. It depends on exactly what your prospect wants.

Sadly, many advertisers don't even know what a decent offer *is*. I'll give you a good definition: **an offer is a reason to buy. It can be anything: a low price, unusual products, a special sale, special bonuses and extras — all the things you're offering to the customer in exchange for the money you want them to give to you.** Too much of the advertising out there doesn't have any real offer attached. People are spending their good, hard-earned dollars running this advertising — and they're not really trying to *sell* anything. They're not giving their prospects a clear and compelling reason to come do business with them right now.

In creating an offer, you should ask yourself what the prospect wants. If you're a restaurant owner, what do they want when they come into your restaurant? Let's say, for example, that you want to make a special offer for Valentine's Day, and normally you'd do "two-for-one," or you'd offer a free dessert, or something like that. Those aren't really eye-popping offers. Instead, think deeply about what your customers *really* want on Valentine's Day. They want the whole romantic feel, right? So how about this: you offer a "Valentine's Day Lovers Package." If they come in as a couple, the female of the party is going to get a bunch of roses, and there's going to be free champagne and there's going to be chocolate-dipped strawberries. There's going to be a person going around playing romantic music on the violin. By creating that type of special offer, you're going to set yourself apart from all the other restaurants out there who want that Valentine's Day business. And as I mentioned before, make it a limited offer. Say something like, "There's a limited number of spaces so you'd better act fast, because these Valentine's Day packages will go quickly."

Here's a good idea that my colleague Randy Charach told me

A business is very
similar to a living
organism...

- The marketplace
  is its life and
  livelihood.

- It feeds off its
  market.

- It changes,
  grows, and
  adapts to the
  changes in its
  environment.

- Many outside
  forces can kill it.
  Some slowly.
  Some quickly.

- Keeping it alive
  for a long time
  can be a delicate
  thing.

about. He was going to the same hairstylist quite often, and one day he noticed that she had a little sign hidden behind her box of scissors and some business cards that said, "Please refer me." She asked him, "You're the marketing expert. How can I get more business?" He said, "It's really simple. You can make yourself as busy as you want by doing what I'm going to tell you right now. I hope you do this, because I know it will work. Give out a card to every one of your customers that gives a free haircut, on the first visit, to anybody they give that card to. All you're doing is giving a free haircut once to one person."

Now, that's going to attract a lot of people to come for a free haircut. She does a good job, her price is reasonable, she's nice to talk to, and there's no reason for them not to come back. The only reason they may not even take her up this offer is that they're afraid to leave whomever they currently go to. That isn't the case with most people.

See? You don't have to spend much money to get good results from Direct-Response Marketing. If you can spend money, that's fine — maybe it's more profitable for you to do that. **You can afford to sell something for $50 that cost you $70, if you know the lifetime value of your customer is $1,000.** You've just got to do the numbers. Direct Marketing is psychology and math, that's all it is: figuring out what the people want and then calculating the metric. Most advertisers don't bother, just as they don't bother to build a decent customer list.

Summing It Up

There's a lot of money out there that's just lying on the table — and it's waiting for you to pick it up. This chapter shows you the tip of the iceberg regarding what Direct-Response Marketing can do for you. So let this be something that whets your appetite, and gets you hungry for more. By all means, go on to the next chapter, but be sure you come back to this chapter and read it again. **Do everything possible to learn everything you can about Direct-Response Marketing, because it's something that can increase your profits dramatically and give you an unfair advantage in your marketplace.**

MARKETING SECRET #15

Almost all profits come from the back-end...

- Spend more time, money, and effort — doing more business with your existing customers.

- 80% marketing to existing customers

- 20% to get new customers.

FREE GIFT: Go to www.RuthlessMarketing.com/freegift

Front-End and Back-End Marketing Systems

In this chapter, I'm going to discuss front-end and back-end marketing systems, and why it's imperative that you develop your own. These systems are extremely important to any business, and if you'll practice the things I'm going to teach you here, you'll benefit dramatically.

Put simply, **front-end and back-end systems are the methods you use to attract customers, and then to sell to them again later.** I look at front-end sales as low-cost hand-raisers that you use as an introduction to new prospects, so they can express an interest in what you have to sell. But every front-end system is created and offered with the intention of making a back-end sale of a much higher-priced item. Your front-end breaks the ice; it's the secret to breaking through your inability to sell high-ticket items to people who don't know you. It lets you make that initial introduction, and identify those who are interested in what you've got to offer.

You should **look at your sales system as a funnel.** You're trying to bring in a large number of would-be buyers and get them into that huge opening at the top. You use a low-cost (or even a *no*-cost) offer to do this, but only to get them acquainted with you and what you have to offer. The back-end is where you really make your money. Once you've broken the ice, most of your would-be customers will fall by the wayside; and that's okay, because you're looking for the wheat, not the chaff. You simply have to take in a huge amount of people to get that small percentage of customers who will buy in the back-end, and then continue to buy from you in the future.

What it all boils down to is this: the front-end sale — that first sale at the top of the funnel — is meant to get a prospect on your buyers list. That's all it's for; it's not about profit, although it's nice if you can make a little. This is where a lot of people make their biggest mistake: they think that the front-end sale is the thing they're going for. Perish the thought! That's just to get the prospect to the point of being a customer, and to get their name on your house list. The back-end is the next sale and the next, and that's where you make your money.

That said, your front-end and back-end systems are actually interlocking components of a complex whole — the overarching Ruthless Marketing System that forms the basis of this book. Once again: **with the front-end system you're bringing people into your marketing funnel. On the back-end, you're nurturing the relationship with those people, and helping those people who give you more and more money.** It's a lot like running an automobile. The front-end is the key that starts the engine; it's small, and doesn't cost much by itself. The back-end system is the fuel that drives the vehicle. It costs a little more, but it's what really drives your business.

In the largest perspective, all this is just marketing — part of the package of things you use to attract and re-attract the best customers. **An effective marketing system is one that does it all for you automatically: the front-end automatically attracts the right people, and a back-end system automatically re-sells them.** I see the front-end/back-end interaction as something like the plate-spinning people you used to see on the Ed Sullivan Show, and that you can still see in some carnivals and circuses. They start spinning those plates, and eventually they get 14 or 15 plates spinning simultaneously. Once they're spinning, all the performer has to do is casually walk back and flip the first one, and then the second, and the third, and so forth. They can keep 15 plates spinning with a minimum of effort — but it does take effort, or they all come crashing down. That's how it can be for your marketing, too. **You can put systems in place that attract and then re-attract all the best customers, with a minimum of effort on your part.** Think of it as a kind of self-perpetuating money machine.

In its simplest manifestation, **your front-end is your lead generation system.** It's the process of taking all the prospects out there and determining which of them you can convert to actual clients. **The back-end becomes the continual marketing to those clients already on your customer list.** The marketing is different for those two aspects of business, since the marketing you'll use to get people to try your service is going to be different from the marketing you'll use to keep selling to the same customers repeatedly. Ultimately, front-end and back-end marketing systems are the best way to build business and create cash on demand.

Gaming the System

Like so many of the components of the Ruthless Marketing System, **front-end/back-end marketing is a systemized way to make on-going, automatic sales.** You should always develop your products and services with this approach in mind, because it's so valuable and proven. My good friend Alan R. Bechtold is in the process of developing a new marketing course, for example, and that's exactly how he's going about it. His new course is based on a series of recorded tele-seminars and a live workshop that he recently conducted. He led a whole group of people through this process in real time, and they each paid a princely sum to be a part of the group; but it goes without saying that it was all recorded, so it could be turned into a course for later use.

First, he recorded five preliminary calls. These calls served two purposes. The first was that they helped those people who paid for the original coaching, and kept them happy until the project officially got started. Second, Alan knew, in the back of his mind, that he was creating a front-end product that he could sell for $17

Developing great selling messages is a process — not an event!

- It takes a lot of time, work, thinking, and re-thinking.

- The best ideas develop after a great amount of hard brainstorming and work.

- You must flush-out the best selling and marketing idea.

As Einstein said... "Genius is 99% perspiration — and 1% inspiration."

or $27 — maybe more, maybe less, based on the test marketing — to find prospects who most want to buy the complete course, which he'll sell for a lot more. Now, Alan knows that he'd have very little luck going out to strangers on the street and trying to sell them a course for $997 or $1,499. **But if he sells them the $27 introductory course and follows up with the right pieces, and maybe even a few phone calls, then the sale is very easy** — because he's giving them a chance to get started very inexpensively. Those first five calls and the tons of information on that one CD-ROM make up almost one-third of the course.

Here's a similar example: Video Professor. They have all these information products that teach you how to use your computer, and what do they do? They offer you the basics on a free disk; all you pay is $6.95 for postage and handling. It's a fantastic method that's used everywhere in the business. Similarly, almost every infomercial you see is a front-end offer of one type or another. **Start paying close attention to those offers.** Call up some of them, and express your interest in buying. Listen to what they have on the back-end, because every offer you see for a low-cost product is a front-end offer, a set-up for the higher-priced back-end offer the marketer derives his profit from.

The idea is to **introduce yourself to the prospect by over-delivering on a low-cost hand-raiser that's worth many times**

more than what the prospect paid. At the risk of sounding sexist, **it's a bit like courting a woman.** You may get her attention initially, but you're not going to propose on the first date. Of course, by nurturing that relationship and getting her interested, at some point you can pop the question and expect a reasonable chance of making your "sale." That's what Alan is doing by leading with his $27 offer, and then introducing the bigger course later. His customers are going to be amazed and excited about paying him $1,000 when they think, *Imagine what I can get for $1,000 if I got all this for just $27!* And here's a point to keep in mind: when making a front-end offer of this sort, be sure to charge something to **qualify the prospects.** Otherwise you'll get a lot of people who aren't serious, and some who are will avoid your offer, because they'll think you can't be serious if you're giving it away for free.

Here's something that a lot of people overlook; I've already mentioned it here, but it's worth re-emphasizing. **You have to understand that a front-end sale is simply a customer's entry point onto your house list; it's the subsequent sales that are the source of your real profit.** I can't tell you how many items I've purchased through the mail, over the Internet, or whatever — and never heard from that vendor again. Obviously, they had no idea what they were doing: they were going for that first sale, and that was it. They got my money, they sent me the product, and it was over; they were on to the next sale. They're spending more money chasing new prospects to get that one front-end sale. It's like the two guys with the potato cart, where at the end of the day they lose money, and they figure, "Well, tomorrow we'll just have to sell more potatoes." But you can get by on fewer new potato sales is you'll just implement a back-end system so you can rake in the profits by selling to previous satisfied customers. Do that, and you're going to have a huge, unfair advantage over 80-90% of the advertisers out there.

Catching a Clue

It's a sad fact of life that most businesses — especially

mom-and-pop operations — have no front-end offer to get people in the door. Their philosophy seems to be, "OK, I'm located at 608 Main Street here and I have a sign in the window that says OPEN FOR BUSINESS. That should be enough." Well, that's the wrong approach. You need a front-end offer to get people into your store — or if you're a service provider, a reason to get them to call your business. It should be something that costs you very little, but has a high perceived value. Don't make the mistake of either having no front-end, or of having a shoddy front-end that nobody wants. On the other hand, it shouldn't cost you too much to sell it at a big discount or give it away for free.

If you're a business owner, you have to keep asking yourself, over and over again, **"What's next?"** I think you should even put it on you wall in 200-point type, where you can look at it all the time: "What's next?" When you've got somebody who's interested and passionate about whatever it is you're selling — whether it's knitting supplies or Army boots — those people are insatiable. They'll keep buying and rebuying. It's up to you, though: **the responsibility is on your shoulders to keep dreaming up new things to sell them.**

Most business owners are either out there chasing the next sale, and wearing themselves out in the process, or they're not doing anything. **Remember Russ von Hoelscher's story from Chapter 2,** about the printer who worked in the strip center close to his office? He was always complaining about how there was never enough business. Russ finally told him, "Look, you've got to get some people in — there are hundreds of businesses within a mile of here. Paper them with flyers, go after the business, and be aggressive." But the printer said something amazingly stupid: "Look, pal. I'm open for business. I've got a printing press. If they want printing, they can come to me."

Now, he's on the backside of a strip mall, and he's unwilling to make that effort to sell his product. That's an absolute recipe for disaster, and it's hard to feel sorry for him! But **he verbalized the**

way that most people think, as rotten as that attitude is. That kind of attitude will only work if you've got a printing press back there and you intend to *print* the money you need to survive. Or, hey, you could print your own "GOING OUT OF BUSINESS" sign. Why not?

In my experience, the people who have that attitude are, for the most part, the people who've opened a business because that's what they've always dreamed of doing. They're already going into it with an attitude that they're the king on the throne, ruling over their new kingdom — their business — and the great unwashed masses are just going to come through the door and be thankful that they've thrown the "OPEN" sign in the window. Sorry, that's not the way it works. It's true that there are some people who do that and actually make a profit, but that only works under certain circumstances; if you have a dynamite location and you give good service, you might be able to survive, a least temporarily. But even if you do, you're losing so much more. If you're not serving the customers properly, you're leaving room for someone to come in take them all away.

If, on the other hand, you'll do the things I'm talking about here, **you won't just survive — you'll thrive.** It's easy: offer a great, cheap offer to get them to come in the first time, let them get comfortable with you and understand a little about your business, then hit them with your back-end offer. Try handing out samples, if your business is amenable to that kind of thing. If you've got a hairdressing salon, offer a $5 perm. Once they're in, make sure you over-deliver, and they're going to be back.

Servicing the Client

Even if you have a great front-end offer that you over-deliver on, **you can't count on every customer to come back on his own.** A good front-end system is useless unless you couple it with an effective back-end system, so you can take advantage of that goodwill and sense of reciprocity you've generated with your front-end offer. What comes next is a regular, systematic communication that goes out to those customers and gives them a specific reason to keep coming back and buying from you. **Even the people who know how valuable a customer list is are losing a whole lot of money that should be theirs, simply because they're not aggressively re-inviting their customers to come back and buy from them on a regular basis.**

You see, your customers are (silently) begging to be acknowledged. They want to be nurtured; they want to be responded to. If you take that first order and do nothing with it, then you're doing a great disservice to the customer. So the obligation you have as a marketer is to massage the egos of your customers, and help them give you more reasons to serve them. **So many times we worry about making that first sale, when in reality it's our ability to help our customers improve their lives, fulfill their desires, and solve their problems that's important.** We do that by continually offering them new products, related products, and related services. They may not even know what direction to go in after they've bought that initial product; so if you just pitch them something at that point, they'll probably come back and buy from you again. So what if it costs you a cent for a postcard and a few cents for postage? That's just a dollar or so per customer per year, and those who respond will spend at least a hundred times that on repeat business with you. What business owner wouldn't exchange a dollar for a hundred dollars every day, and as many times during that day as they possibly could?

Now, this goes right back to what I said earlier about what you, as a marketer, should always be asking yourself: "What's next?" The customer is *already* asking that question, even before you ask it yourself. Sometimes they're asking it even as they purchase that first product. In other words, **they're looking for reasons to do more business with you,** and you've got to be able to answer that question instantly.

An Offer They Can't Refuse

The combination of aggressive front-end and back-end marketing works well with just about any advertising medium, from the Internet and direct mail to infomercials. Just combine this method with the other techniques in this book, especially Direct Response Marketing, and you've got yourself a well-oiled moneymaking machine.

In order for this strategy to work most effectively, however, **you've got to start out with an excellent, high-value offer that your prospect will think they'd have to be a fool to refuse.** A lot of us in the business accomplish this by offering a free report or even a free book as a lead generator. If you want to charge a dollar or two for the book, go ahead; most people appreciate things they have to pay for. But in the case of a report, which is really a glorified sales letter, just give it away free. That'll bring a whole bunch of people into your funnel (you remember the funnel, don't you?).

Let's say I'm selling a book distributorship; I'd offer them the distributorship for several hundreds of dollars on the back-end. But like most people who market information products, I use a 1-2-3 approach with most items. That is, 1) to get the people into the funnel, 2) to make a medium-sized sale on the back-end, and then — the third spoke on the wheel is the most important — 3) offer them an even bigger package: maybe reprint or resell rights for a bunch of tapes and books, at a price that could be $1,000 or more.

My friend Russ von Hoelscher has owned a number of retail bookstores. An effective offer he once used was to have people sign up for a $250 free book-shopping spree every month. All three of the stores he operated at the time used the promotion in their ads, and that enticed people in. There was no obligation, and no purchase necessary. They just signed a card and dropped it into a big bowl. But Russ found that with book customers, even browsers — well, they couldn't just come in and drop the card. They'd start looking at the books, and Russ would often get a sale. Another thing he did, when faced with heavy competition from some of the huge conglomerate bookstores, was to give away, at cost, his top ten bestsellers. It was an effective strategy; he never made much profit with them anyhow. **But by giving a discount of 40% off — literally giving them away at cost — people would come in to get the hot books, but then they'd go deeper in the store**. They'd look at some of the other books and audio programs, and often they'd leave not just with a couple of bestsellers, but two or three other items that made Russ a nice profit.

That brings to mind an especially effective front-end/back-end offer that a lot of different businesses can and do use: a low-cost yearly membership that includes a free report or a free product. You see this kind of thing at Barnes & Noble and at large record stores all the time, but it could be used with just about any business. You start out with a good front-end that leads to bigger and bigger back-end purchases, plus customer loyalty. When people are members of something, they feel better about themselves and what they're buying. Remember, people want to feel important. It's almost like they're running around with these invisible signs flashing, "MAKE ME FEEL IMPORTANT, PLEASE!"

We all want to feel special. **When you make your customers members of something, or give them some association they can join, the real purpose is to develop them as customers and to**

sell them more stuff. If they're a part of some membership, it makes them feel like they have that inside angle or that inside scoop on everyone else. And to a certain extent, they should. You should segment your client list so that your "Gold" or "Platinum" customers get an especially nice deal — for example, a sharp discount, or maybe you open the store only for them on particular days. That can really get some excitement going.

Now, maybe at its root the whole membership thing is phony, since you're more interested in them spending their money than in developing a club — but the more real you make it, the better. Then you're able to educate the customers. If you're selling knitting supplies or beads or books, you can have all kinds of workshops and seminars and bring in book authors to speak. **You can do all kinds of things to get people more addicted to whatever it is that you're selling.**

If you don't have a club for them to join, then have people come in and sign up for a drawing to win a grand prize, the way Russ did. Of course, only one person will win that; but by the end of the promotion, you'll have captured the names of everybody who participated. Remarkably, everyone can be a second-place winner, and get a discount on whatever you're selling! Just send them a little letter that says, "Unfortunately, you're not a first-place winner, but..." and then play up the fact that they *did* win second place. Little do they know that everybody else did too — but that's not important. **Coming in second it makes them feel important; it makes them feel appreciated; and again, it gives them a reason to come back in.**

Here's another thing that a contest does, as it relates to the front-end. **The only people who sign up for any kind of contest are those who are already interested in whatever the prize is that you're giving away.** In my first business, I tried everything to get customers. You name it, I tried it — as long as it didn't cost very much; after all, I was on a limited budget. I used to knock on doors till my knuckles bled. The one method that worked best for

---

The best selling messages and offers grow and develop as you work on them.

- You must take the leap of faith — and develop it gradually as you go.

- Whatever you focus on expands! So keep focusing on improving each offer.

- More often than not, your best ideas will come as the deadline approaches!

me was a giveaway. This was when I had a carpet cleaning business, by the way — several years before I got into mail order and information products. I had a contest that ran continually, to give away three rooms of carpet cleaning, absolutely free. I put these little boxes up in different places around town, and I'd go collect my leads every day. I'd call them up and I'd give them the bad news, which was that they didn't get the three free rooms worth of cleaning. The *good* news was that they'd won the consolation prize, which was conditional. I'd do some free work for them if they would take a minimum amount of other work. Then, once I got in their house, I'd try to run the bill up as high as I could. I was closing between 30% and 50% of all of the people who were signing up for the contest, and the reason **I was closing those people is because they were pre-qualified to begin with.** Only a fool would enter a contest to get three rooms of free carpet cleaning, if they weren't interested in getting that done.

You can always make your consolation prize a lead generation tool, where they get so much off the goods and services you're selling. If you're working with a women's clothing store, like my friend Kris Solie-Johnson, you can run a contest where the winner gets a free outfit, while all the second-place prizewinners get 20% off all their purchases. But you can sweeten the pot a little, too; so why not offer 25%-30 off their purchases if the second-place prizewinner brings in friend who hasn't been to the store before? **Set it up that way, and you'll have customers bringing in customers who are like them,** people you *know* will like what you have to offer — because why would you bring one of your girlfriends to a store if you knew she'd hate the clothes? This can work not only to bring in more customers, but to get everybody back into the store a second time.

You Can't Have a Front Without a Back

Here's something I wished I'd known when I got started: make sure, **once you've got that front-end attractor in place, that you've got something to back it up with.** Once that's system's in place to attract new customers, you've got to have your "What's next?" ready to offer to that new customer as the back-end sale. Let me say this again: you need to have that decided and worked out before you even think about making that first offer to the customer, or your front-end can backfire on you!

The last thing you want to do is to get all excited and worked up about your front-end and then go scrambling to find a back-end to offer your customers. Oh, you can certainly do it that way, but it's a pain. Instead of scrambling when you get that first order, instead of running around trying to figure out what you're going to do, you need to have that already mapped out in your marketing model. You want to put that offer in the fulfillment package for the front-end product. In other words, whatever it is you're using for your front-end sale — whether it's a book or a report or free yarn — when they open that package up, there needs to be that back-end offer staring them right in the face. Because, remember, people are going to be asking themselves right away, "What's next?" And you want to be there with the answer.

That's one of the reasons that I love information products: because you can always use a piece of that information product as your front-end, and you know already what your back-end is. But if yours is a physical product, consider the possibility of planning your front-end offer from the back-end offer. You need your goal — *What am I going to do?* — on the front-end to get them in. What will raise that hand? Now, the worst thing you can do is let that hand-raiser get cold. They're eager to buy *now*. They've just met you, and they're excited about you. They're more excited about you when you deliver that front-end product than they will be for the rest of your relationship, probably. Why on Earth would you wait and let them cool off for three weeks while you think of what else you're going to offer them? You want another offer to go in there — preferably with the front-end package, but if nothing else, immediately following.

Here's another tip: **never have a front-end offer that isn't related to the back-end.** I don't just think that's important, I think it's *essential.* Your front-end offer must dovetail with your back-end approach; otherwise, the person raising their hand isn't necessarily interested in what you're going to sell on the back-end. In fact, in many cases, your back-end can be the same product as your front-end; for example vitamins or supplements. The front-end sale is the product, and **the back-end sale is more of the same.** Sometimes you can get the back-end sale at the same time you make the front-end sale, but that's a whole other strategy.

Think it all through so that **your front-end gives them a small sampling of what they're going to get, so they get to like it.** Be like the Chick-Fil-A or Mrs. Fields cookie people; they're out there passing out free samples. The people who take those samples say, "Thank you" and walk about 20 steps, and all of a sudden they turn around and come back and buy a dozen cookies.

What the Heck *is* a System, Anyway?

Now, *there's* a question that's been begging to be asked: what is a system? By definition, it's a group of interacting or interrelated parts that make up a whole. When you're developing a front- or back-end system, at first glance the whole thing may seem overwhelming; it may seem too complex for you. **The best thing** to do is to look at this system as a set of pieces that all fit together to create, first, that front-end system, and then the associated back-end system.

Your front-end system is designed to promote new products, or generate leads, or sell an order to a first-time customer. But within that front-end system, you may have a series of mini-systems that compose the system itself. Maybe you've got a mini-system that generates leads for your business; then you might have a system in place that you use to create a new offer or new products for customers. Then, of course, you may as well have a system that sells the prospect. Maybe it's your Direct Mail System, where you regularly and systematically contact those leads on a week-to-week or month-to-month or semi-annual basis. (I'll discuss this possibility in more detail in a later chapter.)

The back-end, of course, is the system where the real money really is. It's designed to ethically extract money from the pockets of clients and customers and prospects, and put that money into your bank account — into your own pocket. (Notice, again, that it's important that you do this ethically — if not because you want a clear conscience, then at least because you don't want your misdeeds to jump up and bite you on the ass someday.) You might have a mini-system within your back-end system that progressively and aggressively follows up with your clients every 15 or 30 days. If you do that systematically, you're going to see your sales and your profits grow substantially.

The secret is to bridge the gap between that front-end system and the associated back-end system. The front-end system lets you leverage off your knowledge of your industry, your experience, your background, what you do best; the back-end system lets you leverage off what you know about your clients. It's important that you have a system in place that lets the clients tell you what they want. As the old saying goes, "The only votes that count are the ones that are paid for," and your customers vote by paying for products that you offer on the front-end. You know that on the

Emergency money-making generator...

- When times get hard

- When business gets slow

- When you need cash-flow to feed the monster...

All you do is:

a. Go to your best customers...

b. Make them an irresistible offer!

c. Have a special sale that will blow them away!

They'll stand in line with money in hand!

back-end, you're going to offer them more and more products related to that first purchase.

Most business people are too focused on the front-end, though, to ever make any money on the back-end. They get so excited about making that first sale that it's just like almost being on a narcotics high. But what happens when the sale is over? They've got to immediately go get another high by making another sale. In doing that, they're just leaving money on the table. If they would just work the back-end properly, they could create five or ten times more income and business for their company. You see, **your largest marketing expense is always new-customer acquisition. The easiest business is selling to people who already trust you, who've already bought from you.** Knowing that, you want to create products on the back-end that appeal to those people.

A good example of a back-end system is what happens at Amazon.com. If you go there and buy a book, that's the front-end. But when go through the process of purchasing that book, you're going to see a page that says, "People who bought this book also bought..." Well, that's a back-end offer. Or you may go to a concert, and spend $70 for a ticket. When you get there, they're going to try to sell you a T-shirt, a cap, a CD, or something else. That's the back end. You may end up spending $150 or even more, all told.

The question is, how do you develop a good back-end system? First if all, take a good look at your business. What do you sell to your customers? What are they interested in? Can you upsell them — that is, can you get them to buy something bigger and better? Can you cross-sell to them — can you get them to buy something that's related to that product that you sold them on the front-end? **The ideas you come up with will help you create a back-end system for your business.**

I look at as being it like riding a bike up a tall hill. That's the vision I have of getting new customers. Man, it's difficult! I'm riding that bike up on a hot summer day, and I'm pedaling and I'm breathing hard, and I can't even ride all the way. I actually have to get off and walk the bike up the rest of the way. But then, when it comes to reselling those customers again and again, it's like coasting that bike right down the same hill. I've got my arms up like you do on a roller coaster ride, and I'm not even putting in any effort: I'm zipping right on down the hill. **The fun part of the business is *not* getting the first sale.** The fun part of the business is developing relationships with customers who love you and trust you, who let you get inside their heads and inside their hearts. You get to know them better than they know themselves; and then, whatever you want to sell them, **you create the money at will.**

You've got to realize in business that you're going to spend a certain amount of money to acquire any customer; I discussed this fact in some detail in Chapter 2. All your customers come with a price, whether it's what you spend in ads, or what you spend in time and energy to attract them. But it's worth it if you can figure out the average lifetime revenue of every new customer you acquire. You can literally lose money in the short-term while attracting your customers, if you determine that their value, down the road, is many times more than what you're spending now.

Let me reiterate: *you can afford to lose money on your front-end sale.* You can sell something at less than your cost, if you must. A good 90% of your competition won't do this, because they won't do anything that affects their bottom line. But if you lose a few bucks on the front-end to entice people to come to you, and *then* have great, related items that you can make a huge profit on — then so what if you lose money on the front-end? There's tons of money to be had on the back-end. The most important part of this is knowing what the lifetime value of the average customer is. If you know that, you can go negative on the front-end, because you know that you're going to recover any losses.

Some people call these kinds of offers "loss-leaders." I prefer to think of them as investments towards future profits. If you do everything possible to know your best customers intimately, and make them the kinds of repeat offers that you know they'll be attracted to, you'll make money hand over fist.

But Why Doesn't Everyone Use This Method?

Some people are just too softhearted for their own good to make a system like this work. This all sounds somewhat ruthless — because you're trying to extract every last dollar of disposable income from your customers. But if you're providing products and services that represent true value to your marketplace, then there's nothing ruthless about it. It's more *aggressive* than anything. **I wish more business people would realize the tremendous amount of money they're losing by failing to vigorously resell to their customers.** As a business owner, you should always try to do more business with people who've already shown a certain level of trust in you.

Then again, many business people feel that the high point in their business is getting that first customer. They've never developed the art and science of attracting customers, and they never will. But if you know your system and your customers well enough that you can lose money on the front-end — if you know the lifetime value of your customers, and really nurture relationships with them and help them become not just customers but an integral part of your own life — then there's value there for everyone. The problem with most marketers today is that they only see the quick money, the upfront money, the easy money. They want the get-rich-quick money — when in reality, getting rich is in the *back-end*. It's in the long-term. And hey, let's be honest about it: **a lot of marketers are just flat-out lazy.** They don't want to go through all the necessary steps, and they don't want to take the initiative to do those things that need to be done to make it a business instead of just a hobby.

Another part of the problem may simply be that things have changed in the business world in the last few decades, and people haven't gotten used thinking about, much less using, this new way of doing business. Twenty years ago, if you were the only grocery store on the corner, people went there. Think of it as the Field of Dreams business model: "If you build it, they will come." **But there are so many choices today that we've gotten a bit jaded and cynical about the different marketing messages we see. So the smaller business owner, especially the home-based business, needs to stand out from everybody else out there.** The Field of Dreams business model is mostly dead in America. You have to compete vigorously, and provide additional services that the Big Box companies aren't going to provide.

The key is establishing reciprocal relationships with your customers so your business can survive in the long-term. Let's say you're a novice knitter, and you don't know how to cast off the needles. You're not going to go to Wal-Mart and have someone show you how to do that — because, frankly, they're not going to. You have to go to a smaller neighborhood store that's going to have some of the personal service that the Big Boxes lack, a place that's willing to build a relationship with you. But if they don't pitch to you and don't market to you, you may not know what to ask them. Whereas, if a little knitting store regularly sends you a postcard to tell you they have beginner classes or new types of yarns, **they're educating you,** and you'll probably spend more money with them. Therefore you'll enjoy your hobby more, and they'll get more sales — it's win-win all around.

Hubba Hubba!

Sometimes **it's the worst things in life that provide the best examples,** if only so we can draw parallels to the good things. **So I'm going to discuss pornography** for a while. I realize it's a controversial subject, and I'm going to keep this PG-rated all the way. But there's this story I heard a long time ago; I've never forgotten it, and I think it illustrates something very important when it comes to understanding the power of front-end and back-end marketing. It's the story of Hugh Hefner.

As most people know, Hugh Hefner was the man who started *Playboy* magazine in the early 1950's. At that time, it was a revolutionary idea — though maybe "revolutionary" is the wrong word, because some people are so anti-porn that they may think it was a *terrible* idea. But in any case, it was new; let's just put it that way. Hefner was the first to go this route, and he was very insecure about the fate of his little publication — which, by the way, is rather innocent by today's standards. My wife gets the Victoria's Secrets catalog in the mail, and it's a lot racier...not that I ever look at it or anything!

Anyhow, the first *Playboy* was very innocent compared to today, but at that time it was new and unprecedented. Hefner was so unsure about it that he didn't even print a date on his first publication, since he figured it might just sit on the newsstands for a year or two before it sold out. He printed 5,000 copies, hoping that he wasn't going to lose all his money. But all 5,000 copies sold out in just a few days, and the rest is history.

Some people saw his success and started saying, "Hey, here's a guy who's found a new market!" One of the very first magazines to take him on was *Penthouse*. The story I heard was that when *Penthouse* went into business to compete against *Playboy*, all the experts in the publishing world said, "Look, there's no way this marketplace is big enough for two of these magazines. There's just absolutely no way!" And they did everything possible to advise the people behind *Penthouse* not to do it. "Don't spend your money! The marketplace just isn't big enough for two!" Now, of course, we can see what a ridiculous statement *that* was. Nowadays there isn't just *Playboy* and *Penthouse*; there are about a hundred other publications out there, and some are really quite pornographic.

Here's my point. It has nothing, really, to do with pornography, except as a means of illustration. The point is that **people are insatiable. They can't get enough!** The person who collects one gun is going to have a dozen before long. If there was just one fishing book on the market, that would be ridiculous, because readers would have an insatiable appetite for more — and so there's hundreds of them. The same's true for poker books, and hunting, and stamp collecting. **We're a nation of people who get involved with something and want more, more, more.**

Certain products and services lend themselves more to this emotional intensity than others. Look at casinos. When the government made it so that any Indian tribe in the country could start a casino, everybody said, "Well, there's the end of Vegas. There's the end of Atlantic City." When VCRs first came out in the 1980s, all kinds of people were saying, "There goes the movie industry." When it became possible to download free music on the Internet, all the experts said, "There goes the whole music industry right there. People can get it for free." Well, as you know, none of that has happened. **The marketplace is absolutely, positively** *insatiable*, **and the people buying this stuff from you right now will buy from you again and again,** *if* **you make them the right offers and make it easy for them.**

The problem is that **you have to be creative enough to come up with all kinds of different products and services that somehow relate to what you're selling** — and it really does take some creativity. You can do exactly what Hugh Hefner and all those other guys have done, only you don't have to do it with something like pornography. You can build an empire! You can resell, and you can copy someone who's doing something right. This is especially useful for the small business owner. Find out what your competitor is doing. If he's making a lot of money doing something, you want to do the same thing — only try to do it better than he does. **Don't steal from them, but borrow their best principles.** Even what some people would consider old, crowded markets can be revitalized if you work them right.

The bottom line is that the market is absolutely insatiable. If you grow a garden, next year you'll want to know how to grow a better garden. If you raise a rabbit, you'll like to know how to breed rabbits and sell them to other people. In other words, you — the customer — want to know more. One key to success is *not* looking for the place where there's no competition, but focusing on the place **where there** *is* **competition that's making money in spite of the fact that they don't understand front-end/back-end marketing** — places where they aren't even using those techniques but are still raking in the cash. Now you can step in and dominate that category and they'll be left in the dust, shaking their heads, going, "Wow! What happened here?"

So if you're looking to start a new business, **look for the places where there are plenty of competitors, because that shows just how rabid the market is.** You want to find a market that's not only hungry, but spending money too. Look for people already making money in spite of the fact that they don't know what you know. Let's go back to the pornography example for a minute. My wife once asked me, "What's wrong with men? Don't they realize that when you've seen one picture of a naked woman, you've seen it all?" And she's right — what else is there to see? But this illustrates the fact that people buy for emotional reasons. If everybody thought logically, then you'd see a picture of a naked person and you'd say, "Oh, well, that's interesting," and that would be it. But people can never get enough. While there are certain markets that are more prone to this insatiability, everybody buys for emotional, not logical, reasons. **It's up to you as the business owner to determine what those emotional reasons are, so you can use that as your ammunition and go out and try to get every disposable dollar you can from your customer base.**

There are a few businesses that, at first glance, you might think are *not* emotional — and I've run one. That would be carpet cleaning. But believe it or not, carpet cleaning can be a very emotional thing, because most of my customers were women. Generally, men couldn't care less about whether or not their carpets are dirty; my female customers, on the other hand, were all extremely emotionally attached to their homes. Their homes were important to them, and the more involved they were with social life, they more deeply they cared about what all their friends, family, and neighbors thought. Anybody walking through their home was judging them by the appearance of their home, after all. Once I really got into the heads and hearts of these people, it was so easy to go in there for a $50 job and walk out with a couple of hundred dollars; all I would have to do was point out a few little things here and there. It's all about learning where you can squeeze those emotional triggers.

People buy stuff that excites them more than they buy stuff that they just need. But it's important to point out that they select among the competitors even for those items that they need, and those selections are *still* made for emotional reasons. That's why your message — your offer of a free or inexpensive trial — is important. Now they're getting something for nothing.

Setting Up the Systems

Let's talk a little bit about setting up your own front-end and back-end systems. What I'd like you to do is take out a piece of paper and make three different columns on it. Make one column for low-cost items — typically something that's free or up to about $20-25. The middle column is for items in the $100 range. Make the last column for big-ticket stuff — $500-1000. For every business, you should be able to come up with different ideas about what you can offer in each of these categories, and as I go on, I'll give you examples of brick-and-mortar businesses and how this relates to them.

Next, start brainstorming ideas for different types of products that you put in each one of those columns — because if you set up the system with the back-end *before* you set up the front-end, you'll end up with a continuous flow of products. Once you've got new customers in, you don't have to scramble around trying to figure out something for the back-end. In the beginning, focus on free or low-cost items. The Video Professor example I mentioned earlier is a great one; it's a free CD with information on it — though it does cost $6.95 for shipping and handling. But even though they have to pay shipping and handling, the customer still sees that as a free product. So your front-end offering, at least in the beginning, should be a free or

People want "The MAGIC Bullet":

- The one product/service that is going to make everything okay.

- It's going to solve some major problem.

- Or give them a miracle cure!

- An instant solution!

- And an on-going solution.

If they believe you can give this to them — you will get their money.

low-cost item that's very easy for you to deliver. You don't want to get into something that's complicated to deliver, because that will just eat away at your profit margin.

The second thing you want to **focus on is something that's of very high value to your prospect or customer.** Look at information — maybe insider information. I discussed the usefulness of memberships earlier: about how valuable it is to make people feel important that they're insiders, that they're really part of something, maybe even a part of history. Give them information that can change their business.

I want to make it clear that this isn't the place to give away junk — say, something that wasn't selling very well, or that you couldn't even give away. If new customers start receiving junk, they'll assume that the rest what you have to offer is junk, and that they shouldn't pay any more for whatever else you have. **Your front-end could be some part of a high-end product that you're going to give away,** like the first chapter of a book, or the first few tele-seminars in the beginning of a course. Offers like these really lead people to buy the higher-end product.

After you brainstorm all of these categories, you can start crafting different offers. How can these items work together? What would the flow of one to the other to the next be like? The last step, of course, is finding other businesses that offer your type of product, and studying them for pointers.

Let me give you just a couple of examples of good front-end/back-end systems I've heard of recently. A local library offered a summer reading program for kids, and if the kids read so many books they got a free cookie at a place called the Great Harvest Bread Company. Since the librarian tells kids that they get this free cookie if they read books, they not only read the books, but they become a pain in the butt to their parents to go get that free cookie. When the parents take their kids to go to get this free cookie, they can't just walk into the Great Harvest Bread Company and ask for a free cookie. They have to buy a loaf of bread, too. The bread is $3.50, so suddenly that "free" cookie has cost them cost them $3.50. And if the Great Harvest Bread Company took their names and addresses at that point, they could continue to offer the parents different products by mailings — and the parents might listen. After all, they know where the store is; they've been there before. The people there were nice to their kids — they gave them free cookies — so the parents will probably continue to go back.

Here's how the front-end/back-end worked in this example. First they got the customer in with free cookies, then they upsold to the $3.50 bread. Now it's time to move up to the mid-category, the $100 range. That may be something like a year's supply of bread that the customer pays for at the beginning of a 12-month period. Maybe it's a membership — a "Bread of the Month" Club. There may also be other things they can try to get that customer to give them more and more money, as a result of their initial "free cookies for kids" program.

As you can see, **there are many different things out there that businesses can do to generate business.** If you start mapping out, in the beginning, some of the low-cost, mid-cost, and high-end things that you as a business owner can offer people, you can quickly create a good, step-by-step path from beginning to end, so you're not trying to come up with something all of a sudden later.

Here's a handy tip: **be sure to get it all down on paper.** So many times we try to internalize these things and juggle them in our minds, when really the best thing is to document it all. Create a flow chart of how the different elements of the system are interconnected. What makes one work? What makes it work better? Then you can see the flow of money. If you're constantly creating value, you're constantly going to be getting maximum income from each of your customers.

Here's another thing. Unless we put something on paper, it may be that everything I'm saying here just sounds like a great idea.

You're going to read this chapter, it's all going to be somewhat entertaining to you, and then you're just going to forget about it. For this to work, you have to document your strategies and implement them. My best advice for implementation is to do what I've been trying to do for a number of years: get up every morning and try to focus on your business before all the workaday interruptions get started, before all the distractions get in the way. **Try to think these things through, to develop a plan. Use these very clear, step-by-step strategies to do it, and for goodness sake, write it all down!** That's the best piece of advice I can give you.

A Backup Back-End

One of the most useful things about mapping things out in detail and documenting them is the fact that you can include a plan for those people who won't take you up on that first offer — a backup back-end offer, if you will. Maybe it's a lower price; maybe it's got more bonuses or more value than your other offer; maybe it's something related, but in a sub-category in a different direction. In a week or two, after you've seen whether your customers have responded or not, **you can take those same people who raised their hands in the first place and give them another shot at doing business with you. You know they're going to want to do business with you, because they're pleased with what you over-delivered for the $10 or $20 they gave you to start out with.** You don't want to let them sit too long and forget who you are. I think it's a good idea to make sure your plan branches out. Make contingencies. If they *do* buy your backup back-end offer, do you then send them a higher-end offer, and when? If they don't buy that, do you send them another offer that's going to move them into the funnel better? More to the point, if you have multiple items in your low-cost and mid-cost categories and one isn't working, you can try another.

In any case, **it's important to keep going after them.** You might think it's a pain to keep getting postcards from the same realtor, over and over, month after month — but when you're ready to sell the house you're living in, who are you going to call? Probably the agent who sent you 25 or 30 postcards over the years. So don't give up. Keep sending; stay in touch with your customers, because the more you stay in touch with them, the more likely they are going to respond to you if you have something they want. And make them specific offers every time. You're not just staying in touch with them, asking them to call you for no reason; **you're telling them *exactly* what you want them to do. You're telling them *exactly* what's in it for them. When they do respond to you, they're doing it for a very clear and compelling reason.**

The best part about all this is that once you've got them with your front-end offer, it doesn't matter if you're not the best copywriter in the world. At that point **your copy doesn't have to be perfect,** because you already know they're interested in what you have. Chances are, they're going to want more of it — they're going to be asking, "What's next?" So don't worry about being a world-class copywriter; just whip out a sales letter talking about your next product and send it to them, because you've already broken the ice with that front-end offer. I've said it before and I'll probably say it again: good enough is good enough.

The Sum of Its Parts

There's an old marketing question every business owner should ask himself: "Am I in the business of making sales?" And the answer is: No, **you're in the business of building relationships with customers.** When you develop that relationship, you'll have a pool of customers ready and eager to buy whatever it is you have to sell. Isn't that worth developing a front-end system?

The answer is yes. Earlier, I mentioned the fact that a lot of business people are lazy. Well, if you're lazy — and we all have that streak in us — then you should be excited about what I've gone over in this chapter, because doing well in this business is really about developing relationships. The front-end — the things you do to attract the best prospects, those who are most likely to end up doing business with you in the future — is just the beginning. It's a necessary evil, and it's a lot of hard work. But then comes the real business of making money: the back-end business, where you're building relationships. **For those of us who are lazy, this is the easiest money you'll ever make** because all you're doing is being a friend. People will do things for their friends that they won't do for anybody else; when somebody has a relationship with you, there's a trust built up there. They'll do whatever you ask them to do, as long as they trust you enough and as long as they believe in you enough. Really, that's all this is about. It's the easiest money you'll ever make in your life.

MARKETING SECRET #23

MARKETING MAXIM: You can tell everything about a person — by simply paying attention to what they spend their money on.

- People reveal their true selves — by the way they spend their money.

- "It is where a man spends his money that shows where his heart lies." (A. Edwin Keigurn)

- This is why 2-Step marketing is so powerful.

Work *On* Your Business, Not *In* It

In this chapter, I'm going to teach you how to work *on* your business rather than *in* it. That may seem like a minor semantic distinction, but it's actually what separates the big dogs from the whimpering puppies. Too many business owners out there — the puppies — spend all their time and energy working *in* their businesses. They come home tired and stressed-out every day; they have stomachaches; they're always short of money, they're always tired, their businesses don't work, and they end up going broke. **The smart people out there are the ones doing everything possible to focus all their time and energy on the things that bring their businesses the largest amounts of sales and profits, while delegating everything else.** That's what working *on* your business, rather than *in* it, means.

While it may not seem to be the case at first, working *on* your business rather than *in* it is where this whole outlook gets truly ruthless. Why? Because that tired guy I was talking about in the opening paragraph, the one who's always constantly struggling to keep up, and the bank isn't full, and he has no time, and he's exhausted... well, he's already got two strikes against him. How can he keep an eye on his competition? How can he have the time to devise the next neat trick to out-step and out-sell them?

The key is systemizing your business: building it into something that runs itself. **This frees your time up not only so you can continue to build your business, but so you can enjoy life too!** I love the ruthless aspect of waving at that poor schlep who's still working his business — working *in* it and not *on* it —

as you go by him in your yacht. That's ruthless, because you've got the free time and you've got the yacht — and he's got 12 more hours of work today, and an empty bank account. Working *on* your business instead of *in* your business involves the creation of a business that serves, rather than *consumes,* your life. **When you work *on* your business, you're creating systems and setting things up so that other people can do what needs to be done for you,** without going through major training and facing a steep learning curve — because everything has been documented properly.

You need to take everything that you do more than once, document it completely, and put into a manual. That way, you don't have to reinvent the wheel every time somebody new comes into a task. Even if you're an individual working alone, you still want to do this, so you don't have to go through the whole thought process and difficulties of re-creating everything from scratch. Take emails, for example. You can set up templates for emails, letters, even scripts. **Everything you do can be broken down and made easy for you or someone else to do. Then you can focus on the important things in your business and in your life.**

By doing this, you have several advantages. Not only can you put your focus on more important things, but if you ever want to sell your business, you now have a nice neat package that has more goodwill (in both the social and financial senses of the word) than it would have if you hadn't documented everything. Also, if you decide to expand, you can pay less for new employees, because you can get people with fewer skills. They may still be good, qualified people, but because everything is all laid out for them, you don't need to find people who are completely innovative. I like to look at McDonald's as an example. They have everything down to a "T;" that's why they're so uniform all over the world. You go and get a Big Mac, and in Japan it's the same as it is in Canada or anywhere throughout the U.S., because they have systems for everything they do. That lets them bring people in at a relatively low wage. They do put them through training, but they're training them based on pre-existing procedures and manuals. When you do this yourself, you'll tap into a great sense of freedom.

You see, your employees don't have to be entrepreneurs: that's your job. When you're working *on* your business rather than *in* it, **they're the craftsmen, the engineers, who help move your business forward under your guidance.** You've got totally different perspectives, totally different responsibilities, totally different objectives, totally different accomplishments in your lives. There's a difference between being a craftsman and being the business owner. You've got to run your business, and as a business owner you *must* have the ability to make a lot of money.

Over the years, **I've learned that working less in my business is the smartest thing I can do — and I happen to know that many of my fellow marketers feel the same way.** My friend and mentor, Russ Von Hoelscher, usually works from about 10 AM to 4:30 PM at his office. People who don't know him too well say, "Gee, Russ, you've got the life of Riley! You work only five or six hours a day, five days a week." But you see, it's not true — because he works at least three hours a day at home. He's found that it's a good idea to get up early in the morning and get to work on the advertisements, letters, and issues that concern his business. Once he gets to the office, his employees bring him all the hassles. They're mostly little hassles, but there are always problems he has to deal with himself — some of which do, admittedly, help to build his business. But **most of the real satisfying work to build his business, to make his business profitable, comes when he works at home. When he goes to the office, it's just to manage the business.**

A lot of businesspeople today manage their businesses *all the time*. **They're no better than employees. They may be managers, but they're not really entrepreneurs.** To be an entrepreneur you've got to get away from your business, or set aside time at your business when no one can disturb you while work on those issues that will build your business.

Build "Risk Reversal" into every offer.

- Risk Reversal is taking all the pressure away from the prospect or customer...

- It is an irresistible guarantee

- It's a dramatic promise that they must gain a major benefit — or they not only get their money back — but they will also receive something of tremendous value!

- This blows them away — and will get you a lot of attention and interest.

One of the things that really motivates most business owners, at least initially, is the fact that they're tired of working for someone else. They see an entrepreneur out there who's living what they think is the life of Riley — but they don't understand exactly how they got from Point A to Point B. **Many people start a business with great intentions, but then they get mired in all the little stuff. They quickly find they're swimming in all this minutia that has to do with running their business.** They find it hard to disengage, often because they've been taught, "If you want something done right, you have to do it yourself." But that's not what an entrepreneur does — not for everything, anyway.

You have to realize that there's a whole different set of rules that you need to focus on as an entrepreneur, and having to deal with mundane tasks gobbles up the time you need to be focusing on your business. So how do you get out of that rut? How do you get out of being so immersed in your business and so caught up in small details and little hassles that you really don't have time to focus on your business? You'll find a lot of good tips on how to do that in the rest of this chapter.

That Good, Honest Cliché

It may sound like something that you'd see in a Dilbert cartoon, but the fact is that **working *on* your business and not *in* it is all about working smarter, not working harder.** Hey, it's a cliché because it's true! **One of my favorite quotes is from the great Abraham Lincoln, who once said, "If I had three hours to chop down a tree, I'd spend the first two sharpening my axe." That's what working smart is all about!** Think about it. If you had three hours to chop down a huge tree, and you sat there very calmly and quietly sharpening your axe for two of those hours, you'd get the tree chopped down with a lot less effort. Ultimately, that's what we're talking about.

Here's a list of nine basic things you can do to work smarter, *on* and not *in* your business.

1. **Focus on things that increase your sales and profits,** such as developing and promoting new products and services.

2. **Spend time planning, scheming, and plotting,** coming up with new kinds of strategies to do things better, and ways to serve your customers better.

3. **Work on a new promotion: either to attract new customers, or to re-attract old customers.**

4. **Think about your competition** — even do things to spy on them. Think about all the things your competitors are doing right, all the things they're doing wrong, and how you can do it better.

5. **Spend some time trying to deepen your understanding of your customers, and thinking about ways to strengthen and solidify your relationships with them.** How can you do more business with your customer? Write that question down, spend a half-hour every day answering that question, and I promise great things will happen.

6. **Spend some time planning your day, week and month in advance.** Don't just wake up in the morning without a solid plan. You need to spend some time trying to determine the maximum use of your time, for maximum productivity. And I can tell you this: **when it comes to time management, the more stuff you have planned to do every day that will serve the company and make you money, the more productive you're going to be.**

7. **Spend time dreaming, goal setting, studying marketing materials, and just thinking.** Think about where you want to go, what you want to accomplish, and how you're going to accomplish those things.

8. **Develop information products designed to establish your credibility** and position yourself as an expert in your market. Information products are a great way to attract the best prospects in your marketplace.

9. Combine different aspects of what I've been sharing with you. **Ask yourself the tough questions that none of your other competitors are asking themselves;** sit down and really try to figure out the answers to questions like,

   ✓ "How do we attract and re-attract the very best customers in our marketplace?

   ✓ What do we have to do to do this?"

   ✓ **"What do the best customers in our marketplace want that nobody else is giving them?"**

   ✓ "Where are the untapped opportunities right here in front of us, right now, that nobody else can see?"

   ✓ "What could we be doing differently that could make a bigger impact on our best customers and help them do

FREE GIFT: Go to www.RuthlessMarketing.com/freegift

even more business with us?"

✓ **Here's a great one: "How can I steal the best customers away from my biggest competitors?"** If you could find a way to divert those people over to your customer base somehow, you can claim money that's right there for the taking.

✓ **Another good question:** "What are the three things we can do right now that will dramatically increase our sales and profits?"

✓ How can you cross-sell to more of your best customers?

✓ How can you get them to buy more of your stuff, for a larger amount of money each time?"

✓ **And, last but not least, another great question that will lead to lots of interesting answers and more questions: "What are the innovative companies, both in and out of my market area doing that I can imitate?"**

These might be companies you wouldn't even think of as competition, because they don't sell the same exact types of products or services — but they're doing innovative things that you can adapt for your own business.

If you just spend some time every single day sharpening the axe, thinking very carefully about the answers to these questions, some days you're going to get some great answers. Some days you're not going to get any answers. But keep a notebook, think and dream and scheme, and keep asking the questions, and you'll be surprised at the answers you'll come up with.

Now, you might think that nothing in those nine topics sounds particularly ruthless — but applying them properly is what makes you a ruthless marketer. It's all about focusing on what's really important. I hope you, the reader, are willing to incorporate all these points in your thinking.

One of the most important points I've mentioned here involves how you can sell more to your existing customers, especially your best customers. Most businesspeople focus on one thought: "How do I get more customers?" While that's always important, it's more important to say to yourself, "OK, I've already got "X" number of customers. How can I sell more things to these customers?"

Why is this more important than acquiring new customers? Because I've found the 80-20 rule works. That is, at least 80% of all the profits you make will come from 20% of your customers. It's okay to go after new customers; we have to do this. But **98% of businesses aren't selling enough to their present customers.** If you can create new programs, new products, new services, and new ideas to enhance the business from the customers you already have, you're way ahead of the pack.

This includes what I've referred to as "stealing other people's customers." That's ruthless, sure, but how else do you build up your customer base? Now, **there are companies out there that are doing such a great job of serving their customers**

that there's not a damn thing that you can possibly do to steal them away. My best example of that is my printer. I've got such a great relationship with him — and we do millions of dollars worth of printing every year through his company — that there's no way any printer could ever court me away from him. Ever. He's just doing too good a job; he's serving me too well.

But that's an extreme example. **A lot of businesspeople are getting less than desirable service, and they're less than happy with their present suppliers.** They just get into the habit of doing business with the same companies over and over again, because they don't want to change. **Those disgruntled customers are the ones you can steal.** As I taught you back in Chapter One, part of developing your overall marketing strategy is to create a Unique Selling Position in the marketplace that answers the problems your potential customers are faced with, whatever they might be. If you know what those problems are, you can develop advertising that's aimed at those people, and you can let them know that your company is built to answer and address those issues — whereas their existing suppliers aren't. **The more you know about your very best customers, then the more you'll know how to attract other customers that are just like them, and many will come from your competitors.** A buyer is a buyer is a buyer, so the more you know about *your* best customers, the better you'll know your competitors' best customers too, and the more you'll know about their dissatisfactions. You should also get to know *your competitors.* **Go out and buy everybody's stuff you could find, not just to see what your competitors are offering, but also so you can understand their sales processes.**

Here's another way to make your customers happy, and make more money from them in the long run: just give your best customers a better deal. My friend Russ von Hoelscher used to do business with Staples for office supplies, and also whenever he had to print up 500 copies of this or 1,000 of that. That amounts to a substantial amount per month. Then Office Depot opened just four blocks from him, and he went down there and said, "You know, I do a lot of business with Staples and they give me 10% off their regular prices on all printing and some of the office supplies." The manager was called over and he asked, "How much do you do?" Russ said, "Oh, about three thousand a month. I take my major business to a big printer, but I do a lot of small-scale printing and I buy plenty of office supplies." Well, the manager knew a golden goose when he saw one, so he said, "Look, we'll give you 20% off if you do that type of volume every month." So now Russ is one of his best customers. You can do things like that for your best customers — you can treat them special. When you do that, you can steal 'em from the competition.

Always Remember, and Never Forget...

One of the most important things you should remember with this kind of marketing is that **you absolutely have to take the time to study and think in order to come up with the right strategies. Don't get so wrapped up in those everyday business details; slow down!** Ask yourself the questions I said you should ask yourself in Point Number Nine on my list. When you ask yourself those questions, answers will eventually come. One good question I'd add to the list is this: "What do my customers really want?" I don't care if you're selling shoes or printing or you run a restaurant, what do your customers *really* want? Because it's always above and beyond the obvious. When you start answering that question satisfactorily, you can serve your customers much, much better.

Ask yourself the questions, and the answers will come — and over time they'll better. That's the big secret. I think **the reason a lot of people *don't* ask the questions is because they're afraid. Well, guess what? You'll get some wrong answers. There's no doubt about it. But through the process of asking and answering questions, you'll eventually come up with better answers — which will lead to better questions, which will lead to better answers.** I think a few other questions that are really nice to ask yourself as you're working *on* your business and not *in* it include, "Where are my biggest strengths? What do I have to offer that other companies can't or won't? How can I do better at the things I'm already good at and delegate the rest? What am I spending my precious time and energy on right now that someone else could be doing as well or even better than I'm doing? How can I produce bigger sales and profits with less time and work?" That last one's a good question, because too many people are working their asses off and they're not getting nearly what they should be getting. Or ask yourself, "Who in the marketplace is making the largest amount of money?" And, "What are they doing that I could be doing?" Or, "What are they doing that I could be doing *even better*?"

All this boils down to making a short list (no more than ten) of the activities you can perform consistently to bring in more sales and profits every day — and then delegating everything else to the most competent people you can find, so you're not trying to wear all the hats. **What you're doing is trying to put your time and energy into the smallest number of things that bring you the biggest results.** Assuming you can find the most capable, competent people, you're letting them do what they do best while you're focused on what you do best. It's a much smarter way of doing business than most people will ever come up with. I often ask myself, **"Why don't more people do this kind of thing?"** All I **can think of are these six things:**

- **They're just lazy**.

- **They're delusional.**

- **They just don't know what to do.** If you read this chapter and take it to heart, you'll be ahead of them because you'll know exactly what to do.

- **They're just following the follower**. They're just doing what every other business in their markets is doing — it's the blind leading the blind!

- **It doesn't fit our great American Judeo-Christian work ethic.** People think that if they're not working hard physically, then it's not work. It really *is* work, but it's the cerebral kind; you might get a headache, but you're never going to break a sweat doing any of this stuff. A lot of people feel like they have to work hard and try to do everything at once — and if they're not really tired, then they don't feel like they've worked that hard.

- **People are miseducated.** They don't even know what they need to know, and in fact they don't even know what they *don't* know. For example, many people think of location as the most important thing for a business, but it's not. Location is important for some types of businesses, but that alone will only get you so far. **Most people don't realize that if you use some of these strategies and techniques I'm talking about, you can double and triple your business regardless of location.**

That's the gist of the "work smarter, not harder" argument. The people who are making the most money are doing these things, and I'd like to include anyone reading this book in that category. I'm practicing what I preach, and so are all the other top marketers out there.

What You Absolutely Must Start Doing, Today

In this section, I'm going to share a few tips about what you absolutely *must* be doing if you expect to work *on* your business and not *in* it. These tips can make all the difference between living the good life and actually living *for* your business, which is exactly what you don't want. Nobody I know of wants to live *for* a business. It's a job at that point, and you think to yourself, "I've got to keep doing this to survive." Instead, you have to put your business on autopilot, and systems and planning are key to doing that. Simply put, the truly ruthless marketer hires the best people to do everything, or out-sources wherever possible what he can off-load from his own plate.

The biggest problem I see, when someone is starting out in a business, is that they end up wearing all the hats — and that puts them between a rock and a hard place. They think, "I don't have any money to hire people; gosh!" and, "When do I know to let go of that?" **Obviously, it very tough to let go of tasks when it's your business. I understand that; I've been there. It's your baby. It's tough to let somebody else come in and give the baby a bath. It's tough to let somebody else take your baby for a walk in the park. But you know what? Maybe it's more productive if you do.**

You can't do it all — period. I don't care how much you're good at. You can't possibly provide, for example, the same quality of Web design for your business as someone who only does Web design all day long, day in and day out. Even if you're a Web designer, even if you're a great graphic artist, if you're also paying the bills and running the errands and doing everything and whipping out whatever you can, your work is more hurried. It's not going to be as good as your best. You can't provide the same quality of customer support as someone who does only customer support all day can. You can't even sell better than someone who sells all day — and that's a tough one to take, because most of us feel we're the best person to sell our own business. But if you're the salesman for your business, you're selling yourself short. **You need to be building the business, building new products, and you can't build your business consistently if business building is just something you do in between all the other chores.**

If you haven't already, *immediately* hire someone or find outsourced labor to replace the repetitive tasks anyone can be trained to do. As I pointed out earlier, you should **document your repetitive tasks so someone else can step right in and do it from there. Off-load your workload as soon and as often as possible — and continually re-evaluate everything.** Once a month, here's what you should do: list every task you do every day for a week. Create an hour-by-hour log. Put an asterisk beside everything you did that will build the business and increase revenue, not just save you a few bucks because you did it yourself. Put a plus sign beside every task you did that *someone else* could be doing right now just as effectively. I bet you'll find that you've marked a lot of the same tasks with both symbols. Once you've done that, figure out if it's more cost-effective to have someone else do those tasks.

Here's what you need to remember to figure that out. Even when the money doesn't seem to be coming in to cover it, realize that **your time is the most valuable asset you have in your business.** Add up your business's total revenue. Divide it by the hours you work. You're the driving force behind this business. This is how much each and every hour of your day is worth. Now, maybe you'll find out that it's easier to put some more plus signs on that time ledger. Then make a list of all the things you need to be doing that you're best at that will generate more sales, revenue and growth for your business — but that you never seem to have all the time you really need to do. Calculate how much money you're losing by not doing this, then move out those repetitive tasks that could be done by someone else and make more room for the profitable tasks that you don't do enough. Remember, **you can always generate more money, but you can never generate more time.**

All it takes is a little documentation. Take every repetitive task you do — for example, database entry, building that mailing list, keeping track of who's purchased what — and describe it, step by step, in a few pages of documentation. Put it in a notebook for new hires to read. Outsource graphic arts and Web design work, even if you can do it yourself. Get an accountant to do your payroll and pay most of your bills for you, assuming you bring in enough money to do that. I'll tell you a little trick about outsourcing I've found, too. I sometimes hear people say that you should outsource everything, because employees are a hassle. Well, sadly, nobody will deny that. But I've found that there are certain situations (and it can sometimes be tough to decide which those are) where it's good to have someone in the office with you working, not outsourced. It's good to know they're going to be there tomorrow.

Caveat emptor: outsourcing can lead to some disastrous results, so you want to be careful with it. And here's something extraordinarily important that someone told me a long time ago that's helped me a great deal. I've never forgotten it, and I'd like to pass it on to you. It's just this: **never, ever delegate your marketing to anybody else. You can delegate everything else.** Accountants are a dime a dozen; good employees are harder to find, but you can find them. **And by "marketing," I don't mean selling. Selling is only part of marketing, and you can find salesmen to do that.** In many ways, selling is where they're repeating your marketing on a script page, doing the repetitive part of selling and following the steps you've created to close a sale. That's the manual labor part of it, where you can train somebody to sell either by phone or out there eyeball-to-eyeball, belly-to-belly with the customers. **What you have to do is develop the strategies and methods to attract and re-attract the best customers, to create the advertisements you need to use, the marketing messages, the *ideas* you use to create new products and services.**

Marketing is all of the things you do to go out there head-to-head with your biggest competition and win. Those are the

things you *don't* **want to delegate, because they're too valuable.** At the same time, those are often the very things you'll find that you wish you had more time to do. Those are the things that get pushed aside all too often. Those are the things that get ignored because you get busy in your business, rather than standing back and running your business. There's a big difference between running a business and having it run you. **If you free up all your time to do nothing but marketing your business and creating new products, your business will do nothing but grow.**

I know how hard it is to start delegating all those things. If you're focused on really building your business, you'll find that while it may seem expensive the first time you take an employee in or when you outsource a copywriting job, it's more costly *not* to do them. **If you're stuck writing your own checks or putting out fires instead of marketing, then you're doing the wrong thing.** You ought to evaluate what that's costing you compared to what it would cost to get someone to do it.

Here's an example. I met this copywriter who did some work for our company about ten years ago, and at first I didn't like him at all. He's a famous guy out of Orlando. I won't mention his name, but he's got a limousine that takes him everywhere. He's a little tiny guy and I started out thinking, "What an egotistical monster. I don't want to do business with anybody who's got a bigger ego than me!" But then I found out that **all the time he was getting chauffeured around in his limousine, he was working his ass off. He was writing copy, coming up with all kinds of ideas. He was on the phone with clients, and he was making maximum use of his time.** That's when I decided that I'd prejudged him wrongly; because that's exactly what I'm talking about doing here: freeing up your time so that it's best spent doing the handful of things that produce the biggest profits. He didn't even want to bother driving himself around; it was more profitable to have someone else do it. And there's another point in this guy's favor: doing this was helping further the image that he wanted to create. He makes himself seem rich and successful, and all of a sudden his value goes up!

I know how hard it is to take off some of those hats you have to wear when you first start out in this business, especially since it can cost you initially. But if you just reassign some tasks to other people and apply the extra time to your marketing, you'll soon see much more coming in than what you're spending to off-load those tasks. Your revenue will grow to cover it. I'd bet money on it.

That said, **don't confuse delegation with abdicating.** That's been the source of some of my worse mistakes. There were cases when I thought I was delegating something, but what I was *really* doing was abdicating — just giving up a task and forgetting it. **Abdication is where you just throw things at people and say, "You take care of all that for me," but then you don't check up on any of it, and you have no way of knowing what's going on. There are no checks and balances built in, and the people you trust could be stealing you blind or doing a terrible job, and you'd never know it until the very end.**

There's a BIG difference between abdication and delegation. I see so many business people making the mistakes that I've made in the past, where I'd try to be involved in every aspect of my business. I spent several years doing this, and at night I'd come home beat-up, exhausted, and my stomach would hurt and I wasn't feeling good. It was all because I was trying to wear all the hats, and I was trying to be involved and micro-manage everything — trying to be a manager more than a business owner. That's a terrible mistake I often see other business people making. Sure, you have to oversee things, and there are some things you may decide you'd rather do yourself. **But you also have to build in the necessary checks and balances, and document everything that's repetitive so that *anyone* can do it. That's the basis of one of the most successful business models ever: the McDonald's model,** the one I talked about earlier. They teach you how to make a burger, and anyone can learn. They even have a Hamburger University where they teach you, "This is how *we* make burgers the McDonald's way." Every McDonald's you walk into, it's the same burger, and that's why. That's a selling point, and it's also a business tool.

My friend and colleague Randy Charach spent six years as Ronald McDonald in a previous life, so he's actually been out to Hamburger U. in Oakbrook, Illinois several times. At the time, there were about a hundred Ronalds, and he was one in Canada, where he lives. Even their shows were all scripted the same, and they had very little artistic freedom — which is why Randy stopped doing it. But it's effective for them and it was fine for him for six years, until he got bored and wanted to do his own thing.

Set down and tell yourself, "I'm going to spend the extra time and effort now to document everything." While it may take you a while to document everything you do, in the long run it's just going to save so many hours and so many headaches and create so many benefits that you'll soon be wondering why you never did it before. Even if you're the kind of person who never wants to let anything out of their control, you've simply got to do this. Once something is documented, you're never beholden to any individual; you never have to rely on somebody to do things right. If you try that, you're screwed if that person gets sick or decides to quit. That could generate a lot of havoc and personal distress, and create problems in your business. Get around it by documenting.

That's a significant part of a mindset that you should put yourself into if you want to succeed. **The mindset you should use is that you're setting up this business so you can franchise or sell it. Not that you necessarily will, but if you have the mindset that everything you do has a greater purpose — and that's to create this turn-key business path you can then duplicate, sell to somebody, or take a year off and have it run itself — you'll be looking at it all the right way.** Maybe you'll never sell or franchise your business, but if you've got everything all documented, the value goes way up. It's also a precaution in case you or your key personnel ever get sick. Document even the most mundane, simple things that you take for granted — like sending a fax, for example. You don't know the experience of the other people who are going to come in and do this for you if you're out of action.

Here's an example, again from Randy Charach, who once owned a toy business. One year he was so ill during the Christmas season that he had to be in the hospital during his busiest week of the year. Back then he didn't have everything documented, so he had to make do with good employees and a lot of telephone calls. You can bet he knows better now, even though he says it was a lesson that took him several years to really understand. Now thorough documentation is his insurance policy in case something goes wrong — and it should be yours, too.

Becoming Someone Else

You need to realize that you're a different person when you're working on your business than you are in all other parts of your life. No matter what you're selling and no matter why you're selling it, when you're developing and growing your business, **the *business* is your product.** Let's look at McDonald's again. The great Ray Kroc built McDonald's from a small family business to the powerhouse it is today. And you know what? His product wasn't hamburgers, and never was! Ray Kroc's product was businesses.

You don't want to get stuck believing that you're selling a product. Let's say you own a dance studio; well, don't think that you're selling dancing. **Your business is a mechanism, a way of bringing in money.** Once you start doing that, you've gone from being a hobbyist or a bibliophile or an engineer to something new — a marketer, an entrepreneur, a businessperson. As such, one of the things you won't ever be confused about — unless you start working *in* your business — is that you're teaching dancing, because that's not what people are buying. People are *really* buying the fact that they'll feel good, feel healthy, and meet people of the opposite sex more easily. Once you understand all that and focus on the needs of the customer, then you find out where people are really going.

Plain and simple, you're a different person as a business owner. To maximize your profits and build your business properly, you have to leave behind all this craftsman stuff, all this engineer stuff that you might have taken great pleasure in in your former life. **When you're a business owner, your product is your business, and you need to optimize that. Like I said before, one way to do that is to work as if you're planning to sell your business, because that forces you into upping your revenues and systemizing everything and making it attractive to other people.**

In addition to being a different person

with different concerns when you're really working on your business properly, your rewards are a whole lot different than when you're laboring *in* your business. You're the one who's really playing the game. Let's say you hire a dance instructor. They're not playing the game; they're getting paid to do it. Sure, they're having a good time and probably for them, at that level, that's really good. But you're the one who's got the juice. You're the one who's living or dying by your marketing efforts. You're the one who's growing your business. You're the one who's boating around in a yacht and riding around in the backseat of a limousine, right? You're the dealmaker. You're the creative entity. Money is what brings all the rewards in, and money is how you keep score!

You know exactly when you need to be doing the most productive things for your business. There's an old book by the famous writer Arthur Haley, who was once an on-the-street salesperson. For him, the most productive time of day was 5:30a.m. to 10:00a.m. He was in the insurance business. During his productive time he'd have meeting after meeting and sign people up left and right. It was afterward that the business took place; the "busy-ness" of making sure the accounting was done, making sure the policies were actually signed out, and getting any questions answered or follow-ups done. That was done in the afternoon, in low-priority time — time when he couldn't be selling anyway, because everyone was at work.

You should do the same, whatever your productive time might be. You know better than anyone the time of day that you do your best work, whether you work best in the morning or at night. Then prioritize the most important aspects of your business. If you get these things done, no matter what else you do (or don't) get done, then the day has been a success. You've made progress in your business in the big picture. How you want to do that is up to you. I belong to what I call the "5 A.M. Club," along with my friend and fellow marketer Ted Ciuba. If I can get up any time at or before 5 A.M. then I've made it. I have other friends who work best in the late afternoon or evening. I know that for somebody like my friend Alan Bechtold, it's impossible to join the 5 A.M. Club, because he's a night owl. He does a lot of his deep thinking at 1 A.M. Like any good entrepreneur, his business doesn't run him, so he can go in when he wants to, and spend at least two hours of writing when he's at his freshest — before he's been distracted, before he knows what distractions are going to pull him away from it. **Most of us get an hour or two of writing in each day, whether it's on product development, ads, or whatever. Some of you guys, as you're starting a business, may only be able to do that for 30 minutes. That's fine. If you can do that consistently and then extend it to a few hours a day, you're going to be so far ahead of your competitors they're going to be freaking out, wondering what the heck you did to by pass them.**

You may actually spend a lot of your time studying, which I highly recommend. There are many courses and information resources and books related to your business. If you owned a pet shop and **got up every morning and spent two hours a day — or even an hour a day** — just reading about the various products and animals and care that you sell in your store, you're going to have the equivalent of a master's degree in five years of reading. Meanwhile, you're going to be learning all about marketing, too. The bottom line is, in the end **you will be a master at what you do.**

Just do the important stuff during your most effective period, and spend your other time taking care of that "busy-ness," fixing up the details that keep the business running, answering emails, doing rote tasks that don't require much thought. If your business is systemized, then you've got it made, and you don't have to do everything yourself. As for me, if I can't run all the business aspects of my business in a few hours a day, then *I* am doing something wrong — and that's just too bad, because that's all I'm going to give it! There rest of my time needs to be spent creating.

What should your priorities be? Anything that sells or builds your business. Studying everything you can about your

FREE GIFT: Go to www.RuthlessMarketing.com/freegift

business. Of course, it's critical that you spend a lot of time in product creation. Production is really what I call it, because it's not only product creation: it's product copy, writing ads, marketing your ads, overseeing your website, making things work better. Product creations and the associated marketing are the big priorities, things you definitely want to carve out time for and do every single day. This is what *nothing else* can interfere with. Everything else, even your other priorities, can slide — but you have to create and market. Here's a suggestion somebody gave years ago that's helped me a lot. **Every single day, do at least one thing that's going to dramatically increase your sales and profits, that stands the greatest chance of bringing you some serious business. That's proactive: it's being offensive, rather then defensive.** You're setting out to do this and to make this happen. If you don't let a day go by without doing something concrete to grow your business, then your business will thrive.

How extensively you want to structure your day is something you'll have to work out by trial and error, and how you do so may evolve over time. Here's an example. My fellow entrepreneur Chris Hollinger used to be a teacher, and he had a lesson plan prepared for every day. Every single day, he knew what topic he was covering and how he was going to cover it. When he became an entrepreneur, he kept that part of his daily routine in place. It worked out well, and kept him on task. But then he started looking at his lesson plans for the business he was putting together, and he realized, "Okay, I'm spending too much of my time on things that I shouldn't spend so much time on." That included things like answering emails and taking care of mundane tasks. So he forced himself to say, "I'm going to make a commitment to free up the time so I can focus on these things that make me the most money. That's what I need to do now as an entrepreneur." As a teacher, it was his classroom; he had to take care of all those details. Now, as an entrepreneur, Chris has a lesson plan for himself that keeps him focused on the times he needs to be selling, and the times he needs to be preparing to sell. He's gotten into the habit of giving everything else up, systemizing it, and having other people do it

Good marketing is a process of:

1. Seeking & finding the people who desire what we sell...

2. Convincing them that we can give them what they desire...

3. And then continuing to give them a wide range of products and services that somehow satisfies their desires.

all. **To do this well requires an awareness of all the things that produce the biggest profits for you in your business, and the willingness to find ways to delegate everything else as much as you can.**

Who Says There Are No Shortcuts to Success?

Within every industry, there are things that you can do in far less time and still receive the same benefit, if only you're spending less time on them. You should look for those shortcuts everywhere. At M.O.R.E., Inc, we've found lots of ways to take shortcuts, and we take as many as we can. Most people don't. I think the reason is this: taking shortcuts sounds like a lazy way to do things. Many people feel they have to work their butts off. What they don't get is the fact that if they can save some time, they can make more money, too! I love what one of my mentors told me early on: he said that **when he goes to the bank to deposit all the money that came in that day, the teller at the window never asks him, "Did you work hard to make this money?" They don't care, and you shouldn't either.** So take your shortcuts. As you get better at the fewer things that produce the largest amount of sales and profits, you'll come up with all kinds of shortcuts. You'll end up spending less time making more money, and probably thinking more. This is a very, very powerful principle.

The Good and the Bad of Having Employees

Employees can be huge assets to your business — but the fact is, they're also big liabilities! You have to be very careful to hire your employees for the right reason — not because they're attractive, or because you feel sorry for them. The responsibility for hiring the right people is *yours*. **It's up to you to make sure you get the right person for the right job, so you have to interview these people and be sure they have the basic skills.** But more importantly, you want a person who's friendly, upbeat, helpful; a people-person, a person with a positive attitude. You might tell someone their job description is A, B, C, but you always want to say, "Look, sometimes we're going to require you to do other things as well." You don't want someone to tell you a month later, "That's not part of my job!" If you have a small business with just a few employees, you need to make their job description very broad, and you need to fill the slot with a person with the right attitude, who's got the basic skills, who's eager to get to work and has a great "people" attitude. It's so much easier to deal with this type of person. Even with good employees, of course, you're going to have some problems; there's no way around that, but you can minimize them if you're careful.

In short, you need folks who'll help you build your business. **A good employee won't cost you money — they'll actually make you money, both indirectly and directly, by freeing up your time and leading you to places you wouldn't have gone without them.**

Giving Good Customer Support

The very best employees to hire are the ones who contribute directly to your revenue stream: for example, Customer Support personnel. Here's a good ruthless marketing principle for you: Customer Support is a chance to sell more. With Customer Support you answer a question and help the customer; you've now befriended them, so they're more apt to buy more.

Every customer contact is a chance to make a sale. If you hire the right Customer Support people, and they're trained the right way, they'll bring in much more money than you're paying them.

A good Customer Support worker also knows how to take an irate customer and calm them down. Perhaps an order was shipped but it didn't get there, and the customer's screaming — well, a good Customer Support worker knows how to settle them, to make them realize you're going to do the right thing for them. They can also up-sell, which is another priceless quality. Keep in mind, though, that **Customer Service is a great example of something you can systematize. You can set up scripts for your Customer Service personnel to work with, whether they're just directing people to the proper department or actually troubleshooting issues.**

Reaping the Whirlwind... Or Not, as the Case May Be

Most of what I've talked about in this chapter boils down making up your mind that you're going to develop the systems and time-saving methods that let you slough off all those boring everyday tasks, so you can do the things that will make you the most money. If you're caught in the hurricane of your business and you're taking care of all the minutiae and putting out fires every day, and it's just killing you, then you have to decide to set goals that bring you back to reality. You might decide, "Hey, I only want to spend four hours in my business and that's all the time I'm going to give it," then spend the rest of your time creating your products, marketing, and enjoying your life. Just make up your mind to develop the systems and all the delegation that needs to go with them in order to focus strongly for four hours on the things you *really* need to focus on. As for the rest, you can be thinking and planning while you're sailing around on your yacht. You're working *on* our business even as you sail — which justifies all the fun you're having!

That's what most of us would want. **There are so many businesspeople who get started with the idea that they're going to make a lot of money, and they're going to have this great new jet-setter way of life... and what they find is, they've just got another job. Only it's the worst kind of job, because your boss is a bastard and you can't get out now.** With most folks, if things go sour on them and they can't stand their job, they can just quit and go to work elsewhere. But if you've built up a company where you owe all kinds of money to all kinds of suppliers, and you've got all kinds of customers you've made promises to over the years, and you've got all kinds of Joint Venture relationships with different people — well, it becomes very, very difficult to just say, "Okay, I'm through!" **You're sort of in prison now — and that's why there are so many businesspeople out there who are anything but free.** They start their businesses with all kinds of hopes and dreams, and they buy into all the hype about how being self-employed is going to lead to all this glamorous stuff. But just a few years they're asking themselves, "Oh my God! What have I done?" They become slaves to their business, and very seldom think about their business on a yacht, because they don't own a yacht!

Now, I'll readily admit that working *on* and not *in* your business is only one strategy for business success, but I think it's the ultimate strategy, because it's more proactive than others. Most businesspeople spend all their precious time doing what I call "putting out brushfires." They go into their company and get sucked into the vortex of it. I used to be one of them, and for several years, that was my life. I was right out there with them, putting out those fires and losing my focus. **Most business owners are just like managers. They're high paid babysitters and really don't own a business: they own a job.** That's a terrible thing, because we start our businesses with the idea that we're going to move away from that whole J-O-B thing... and then we find that we're back in it. You know, if you're in trouble legally, the worst thing you can do is become your own lawyer and try to defend yourself in a jury trial. In the same way, the worst thing most people can do is be their own boss, because it's just terrible.

As a business owner, you tend to stick to what you know. If you're an engineer, you'll probably start an engineering business. If you're a carpet cleaner, you start a carpet cleaning business. Most people think the work that the business does *is* the business — and that's so wrong it's not even funny! *You're in the business of performing the work that you do.* There's a subtle difference, and it's hard to explain sometimes. **The business you're in and the things your business does, in terms of products and services you provide to customers, are two entirely different things.**

Here's a quick example: suppose there's a handyman who all of a sudden gets more work than he can handle, so he gets other handymen to go out and do the work. Then, all of a sudden, he finds he no longer has time to be a handyman, so instead he's booking out all these other handymen. And now he's suddenly in a whole different business: he's now managing people. It requires a whole different skill-set than he's used to. That's not to say that this won't work out, but you're now talking apples and oranges. What worked for you as a handyman or an inventor or as a salesman may not work when you make the transition to marketer. It's what writer Michael Gerber calls the eMyth, in his book of the same name. It's the entrepreneurial myth — the person who's out doing the work all of a sudden shifts into a whole different role and thinks that will work, too — whereas in most cases, it won't.

The point I'm trying to make is that just because you're a good dance instructor doesn't mean you'll make a good dance entrepreneur, unless you throw off that eMyth and learn the skill-set you need to build a business. Always remember: *the function of an entrepreneur is to create money.* If you remember nothing else from this book, remember that statement. Look at the average entrepreneur, and you'll find they have a checkered history: they've been in five, ten, twenty different businesses, because what they're doing is *not* the craftsmanship job. In fact, I believe that Michael Gerber, in his book *The eMyth Revisited*, even makes the argument that **you're better off if you *don't* know how to do the tasks and *don't* know how to be the craftsman and *don't* know how to cook hamburgers or be a dance instructor. And why is that? Because then you can go out and focus on building your business, which is a whole separate function from the actual work the business does.** Your expertise is going to sell more than the competition could ever hope to. Do this, offload all those repetitive, dull tasks and get yourself focused, and you're going to build a wall around your business that nothing can penetrate.

A Parting Shot

As I end this chapter, I want to encourage you, as always, to read it over more than once. Take some notes and do some heavy thinking about all of this. I want to leave this chapter with one idea. The answer to these six words will determine the amount of money that you're going to make. And here they are: What are you willing to do? **If you'll only spend one hour, every day, totally focused on all of the things I've talked about in this chapter, you will be *amazed* at the results.**

MARKETING SECRET #31

The safest marketing
system that
guarantees
consistent sales and
profits:

1. First generate the
   highest quality
   leads you can
   get from space
   ads — or small
   direct mail
   packages.

2. Get the customer
   to request more
   information.

3. Then follow-up
   and hit them with
   all kinds of
   personalized
   sales material
   that takes the
   place of a live
   sales rep.

What Ruthless Really Means

In this chapter, I'm going to tell you what have to do to become a truly ruthless marketer. I'll teach you how to stock up on your ruthless ammunition, how to treat your customers and competitors both, and how to become the center of attention in your marketplace. Along the way I'm also going to tell you more about what ruthless means — which may not necessarily be what you *think* it means. For example, **when I talk about "ruthless" marketing, what I really mean is *aggressive* marketing — it's just that "ruthless" sounds better!** But there's more to it than that, so sit tight, read on, and I'll reveal how you can become the most ruthless marketer you can be.

Positively Ruthless, In Every Way

First of all, "ruthless" isn't necessarily a negative term; a lot of people don't understand that. If you look at the dictionary meaning of the word "ruthless," you'll see that it *can* mean a lot of bad things; for example, somebody who is ruthless can kill a person without a second thought, because they have no conscience. But that's not exactly what I'm talking about here. **Ruthlessness can, in fact, be a positive thing for both you and your customers, though your competitors will never thank you for it.**

In a way, one of the easiest ways for me to describe ruthless marketing to people is by telling then that truly ruthless marketing occurs when we cater to the self-centered emotions of our customers. What I mean by that is this: people buy for emotional reasons. We've covered this before: you've got greed, guilt, fear, pride, and love. Basically, if you think about it, everybody is a self-centered individual living in a mostly self-centered world. From the client-side perspective, ruthless marketing focuses on the emotional reasons people have for purchasing. Yes, you can create a negative situation if you really play to somebody's fear and make them scared to the point where they think they have to have your product to safeguard themselves: "Oh my gosh! I've got to run out and buy that because I'm fearful that my house may get broken into next week!" You can almost slap the consumer around and make them pay attention to what you're saying — that's one way to define ruthless marketing.

Ruthless marketing also means doing things differently than your competition. A lot of people are timid marketers, or they're "me too" marketers: they're only willing to do what everybody else is doing in terms of their marketing. You can't blame those people, because **whenever you get into a new business, the only thing you know to do is to copy the people who are in that exact same business.** So all the Yellow Page ads look the same, and all the mailers look the same, and so do the door hangers and the business cards; it all looks the same. That's timid "me too" marketing. It's not very exciting, and it really doesn't set you apart from your competition.

That's the root of the issue for me. Ruthless marketing means doing things that set you apart from the competition, that get you a bigger market share, more customers, and more profits. **It's the activities that make your competitors fear you, because you're stealing their customers and the money they want.** And you shouldn't think that's a bad thing, because in doing that, you're building a strong business of your own, thereby serving a lot more customers with the best quality products and services possible. Better yet, you're also building up your income for your own dreams for your family.

Again, in this sense, ruthless marketing is a great thing, not a negative thing. When a lot of people hear the word "ruthless," it

FREE GIFT: Go to www.RuthlessMarketing.com/freegift

conjures images of some kind of ruthless pillager — a Viking who just goes out there and takes whatever he wants. In some ways, that's true: as competitive an environment as the marketing world is, sometimes you've just got to do it that way. You have to tell yourself, "Okay, I'm going to do these things in order to capture my market share, in order to make the profits that I want and need to keep my business afloat." Oftentimes we've got employees to whom we have an obligation; we've also got families who depend on us. The ruthless mindset is just a means to an end, in that we're developing the skills that focus on those human factors that get people to give us their money.

The bottom line is, a ruthless marketer is not paid for his *methods*, but for his *results*. **If you're going to concentrate on manipulating and coercing people's emotional factors and psychological frames of reference in order to get them to spend their money with you, well, yes, that does sound very ruthless. But the reality is that it's just part of capitalism. It's part of being competitive, and part of doing what needs to be done to create a thriving marketing business.** When it comes to marketing in general, you don't want to be timid; you don't want to be shy. Sometimes you don't even want to be nice! So when I hear the term "ruthless marketer," I think it's a good thing that's attached to the end of my name. It's not something to be afraid of or ashamed of. It's actually a point of pride for me that I've invested in the skills necessary to become a ruthless marketer.

That said, **let me tell you a little about what ruthless marketing is *not*.**

1. **It's not taking advantage of people.**

2. **It's not lying, cheating, or stealing.**

3. **It's not ripping people off.**

Ruthless marketing isn't all the things you think of when you think of "ruthless" as it applies to a personal attribute. When you're

Don't re-invent the wheel...

Riches are found in re-hashing the best ideas, themes, methods, strategies, and systems — that have produced the BIGGEST profits in the past.

- It's better to re-write a successful promotion from the past — than to come up with something brand new.

talking about relationships among friends, the term "ruthless" might conjure up images you find unpleasant. But when it comes to business, especially when it comes to your competition, it's a necessary mindset. **The ruthless marketing mindset is that there's a whole lot of money out that's being spent, and you deserve to make as much of it as you can get. Your goal is to serve customers and make a profit. One of the ways you do that is by charging in there with the overall mindset of "take no prisoners" — this mindset that you want as big a market share as you can possibly get, and you want make as many profits as possible while playing the game *right*.** It's not about taking advantage of people or ripping them off. It's about having this mindset that, of all the discretionary income out there, you want the largest market share, the biggest piece of the pie. That's what ruthless marketing is all about.

It's more about being aggressive than anything else. When I was a kid there was a rock-and-roll song called, "No More Mr. Nice Guy." I used to love that song! Plus, I like what Carl Icahn used to say: "If you want a friend, get a dog." You've got to be ruthless! You've got to be aggressive! **You've got to develop the heart of the lion and the mind of the fox. You've got to be bold and audacious, and even a little bit cunning, in order to seize the greatest opportunities for sales and profits.** Like I said, it's not about lying to people or cheating them; it's about mastering the art of getting the largest number of people in *your* market to give *you* the largest amount of *their* disposable income.

When you study the secrets of all great marketers, you'll see that they've all got this ruthless marketing mindset: the mind of the fox and the heart of the lion. Your job is to get as much money out of your marketplace as you possibly can. Your job isn't to be friends with your competitors, and it's not to be worried about what other people are going to think about you. I mentioned earlier that most businesspeople are far too timid. At an early age, we learn that it's not a nice thing to blow your own horn and toot your own whistle. We learn at an early age that we shouldn't be cocky or arrogant or egotistical. Even worse, I think there are too many people in this world who have what I call an "employee mentality." **Even people who've been in business for a number of years... in their hearts, they still think like an employee. I don't mean that as disrespectful to employees, because not all employees are alike; but most employees are waiting for other people to appoint them, to tell them what to do.**

When you look at the people who are the most aggressive and are achieving the largest amount of success in the marketplace, you'll see that they're not waiting around for anybody to appoint them to anything. They're out there tooting their own horns or ringing their own bells. Some of them, in fact, set out to be a little controversial. They're not really concerned about what other people are going to think about them. What they're primarily focused on is doing all kinds of bold and audacious, outside-of-the-box, wild and crazy kinds of things that get the best customers attracted to them, because they know their competitors are all after the best customers too. So you've got to do something to completely separate yourself from everyone else, and get all of the money that could and should be yours, and not your competitor's.

On another note, the ruthless mindset is to **treat business as**

a something like a sport or game, as I've mentioned in other chapters. We're in this game to win. It's almost like playing Monopoly. We're not just going to continue to move around the board just for the fun of it. We need to put up our houses, and then put up hotels. That's how we win that game. Ruthless marketing is taking that concept of winning a game like Monopoly into your business. How can you get the houses in the right places? How can you get your marketing in front of the people who need to see it, ahead of all of your other competitors? *We're here to win.* **Never forget that.**

There's an old fable about a gazelle that gets up in the morning. The gazelle has to run faster than the lion behind it — or, at least, it has to run faster than the slowest gazelle, because if it doesn't, the lion will catch it and eat it, and then it's out of the game. The lion, on the other hand, must run faster than the slowest gazelle, or it'll starve to death. It's the same thing in business. When the lion eats up those weaker competitors, you're next in line. If you're the gazelle, you need to get in front of the herd, and the only way you do that is through ruthless marketing. "Ruthless" is really "aggressive." But I also think that **to be really good at ruthless marketing, you need to have courage. Courage is going to put you at the front of the pack in everything you do.** You can't be timid, because then you're that last gazelle, just waiting to be eaten by the next lion that comes along.

Ruthless Ammunition and the Psychological Edge

My friend and colleague Eric Bechtold talks about something he calls "getting your ruthless ammunition for your business." The definition of "ruthless ammunition" is going to be different for every business, so you really need to internalize this and focus on how it applies to your business in order to understand what it means. Basically, Eric's goal in marketing any program or product or service is to put it into his advertising formula. This is where the ruthless marketing part comes in, because first, in order to perform a good marketing push out there, in order to connect with your customers, you always need to try to figure out what the biggest problem is, or the biggest solution you're providing to your customer. **Think about your product or service from your customer's standpoint, and try to figure out how you make their lives easier.**

Let's say, for example, that you're selling car seats for parents to put their little kids in when they're driving to work or school or wherever. You can broadcast a TV commercial that shows the plain statistics: about how 85% of children who are injured in car accidents are injured because their parents didn't put them into the proper seating. To be most effective, you need to focus in on all these scary statistics, and play to their fear for their kids' safety. This is just one example of how you could get yourself into this ruthless mindset, simply by **figuring out what problems — or worries — drive your consumers. Focus on that, and identify those issues. Obviously, the above example is a very specialized situation, but it illustrates the general method. You want to agitate those issues, bring them to the surface, and really get your consumer feeling the pain.** Make them scared. Make them want to say, "Oh man, I really wish I could do that or have this. My life would be so much better." If you make them feel their pain, you can sell them the solution.

That's one example of ruthless marketing, and that's Eric's advertising formula for handling that situation. But there are also other psychological influences that you can play to, factors that influence how people buy. These include:

- Scarcity

- Authority

- Social proof

- Consistency

- Liking

- Reciprocity

These are all things you can focus on when you're searching for those problems that you're going to agitate in order to get people to buy. I've talked about this before in several previous chapters, but it bears repeating as I wrap this book up: you've absolutely got to know your customers better than they know themselves.

There's a book out there called *Non-Manipulative Selling*. I know that sounds like a joke — like it would be a completely blank book, on the order of *Everything Men Know About Women* — but it's not, which I find a little mind-boggling. I can just imagine all these people buying that book who want to be nice people, who don't want to take advantage of others and don't want to manipulate others. But guess what? *All selling and all marketing is manipulation.* **You're trying to get people to spend money with you instead of your competitors. You've got to know all the tricks in the book. You've got to line up your ruthless ammunition and have it ready at all times. Having the best product and service is not enough; the marketplace is unfair in every way. Many times, the people who do a better job of marketing are the ones who are going to make all the money, not the company that delivers the best product and service. That's the reality of the**

MARKETING SECRET #33

People don't want the items we sell... They only want whatever they are led to believe the items can do for or give them.

- Our job is to paint the picture. — We must lead them to believe in some great life-changing benefit.

marketplace. But if you're committed to quality products and services, then you've also got to know all these other little tricks and secrets that other marketers are using to try to get the best prospects in your market to give the money to *them* rather than you.

Take scarcity, for example. I don't think that you have to have one of your products for every one of your customers. That may be nice and fair, but life's not fair. Scarcity is something that moves people to make a decision to buy your product. Maybe there's a limited number of free items you're giving away; maybe it's limited access to consultants. **There's got to be some sort of scarcity that moves people off the couch to come and give you a call.** But it really has to be honest scarcity! You often see those commercials nowadays where they say, "You have to order in the next 30 minutes to get this bonus." You'll see this on an infomercial, and you'll see that infomercial every single night and it says the same thing, every single night. Eventually, no one believes it anymore.

But there *are* some really smart companies that train their customers that the scarcity is real, and if you plan to use this tactic, you have to be like them. Say, for example, you only have 17 of a particular item and a customer is the 18th person, or the 20th or the 50th to contact you. What do you say? Tell them, "I'm sorry, but all those bonuses are gone. We do have these great gifts for you, but all the big bonuses are gone." What you teach them is to respond to scarcity when you put it out there. If you train people to do that, they'll be more responsive whenever you make new scarcity-based marketing offers.

Car dealerships have a big problem with using scarcity tactics; they use them completely the wrong way. A lot of the major manufacturers have special sales, and they're always ending. Then the next week, you see an ad on TV — and the same sale is still going on, or it's been extended, and you find out it's been extended indefinitely — or at least until people stop responding to it. Then they come up with a new deadline or something.

To go ahead and pick on the car industry some more — talk about your ruthless marketers! Car dealers routinely use reciprocity in their message. Have you ever sat there while you're buying a car and the salesman you're dealing with says, "Okay, hold on. Let me go check with my sales manager and we'll see if we can do this for you." He comes back and says something to the effect of, "Well, we were able to do this for *you*." Now, what's that doing in the mind of the consumer who's sitting there thinking about buying a car? It's saying, "Wow, they did this for me; now I should do something for *them*." It's using human nature against that person. "We were able to take $2,000 off this price and give you a better warranty. We were able to do this for you." They're going to be asking for you, the consumer, to do something for them. That's a good example of reciprocity as used in a car dealership. You can use that psychological influence in many different settings with your business, regardless of what it is. All you have to do is identify that it's something you'd want to do in your marketing, and then dream up ways to utilize that psychological influence on people.

Use your ruthless ammunition to declare war against all your direct competitors. There are only two types of competitors: indirect competitors who are selling to the same types of people that you sell to, but aren't selling the same exact products and services; and direct competitors that are selling the exact same things you are, to the exact same people. **Those people are your enemy!** Start thinking about them that way right now. **Learn how to hate them, if you have to — but just as a psychological tool. You've got to see them as trying to take money away that should and could be yours.** I see a lot of people who don't consider their direct competitors their enemies, and I think in some marketplaces, you can afford to have a better attitude about it. But in other marketplaces there are only so many good prospects and customers to go around, and the pond is not being replenished much. If you're not trying to go after those people, you know your competitors are.

You *cannot* be timid about any of this! You've got to be

very aggressive. **If you're timid about it, it's only a matter of time until you hang out your "Going Out Of Business Sale" sign, because at some point a competitor will come along and take all your customers.** I've seen it happen in the small business world over and over again. A business owner sits and says, "Oh, I've got all this business coming in. I don't have to do any marketing. I'm making so much this year." They never figure out that they need to continue to market. What happens is, either a competitor comes in nearby, or maybe they have to move and can't take their customers with them. They no longer have the right storefront, and they just go down the tubes — and they go down fast.

If you're not a ruthless marketer, you need to change your attitude, even if you're doing well — because success is a temporary state that'll last no longer than it takes for an aggressive competitor to come in and take your market share. **You can't just sit back and enjoy life, because business is too competitive these days.** It's no longer a situation where you can start a business, hang out a shingle, and people will come. That's a common fallacy. You need to aggressively, ruthlessly go out and grab customers off the street and drag them into your business. It's the only way you're going to stay in business long-term.

Make Audacious Promises

Eric Bechtold told me once that what "really slapped me around and made me change the way I was thinking ruthlessly," as he put it, was something he heard at a Direct Marketing conference. Someone pointed out that **in every offer you make, you've got to make a bold, audacious promise to your customer — something that you're going to have to struggle like hell to actually produce.** Sure, you're going to have to work really hard in order to fulfill that commitment, but that makes you that much more likely to go out there and over-deliver.

That person also pointed out that, when you make these bold

The secret to
persuasive writing:

1. Know your
   audience —
   what they want
   — what makes
   them tick.

2. Know your
   subject cold.

3. Then don't even
   think — just write!
   Let it flow! Let it
   come from your
   heart — from
   your gut... Let it
   be REAL and
   unpolished.

- You write from
  your heart &
  soul... You write
  with passion and
  energy!

claims, some of your customers aren't going to be 100% happy with what you're offering if it doesn't completely meet their expectations. You have to make it clear to them that you're going to back your promise with a guarantee: so you say something like, "If you do such and such, you're going to increase your business by 200%, or I'll guarantee I'll give you every dollar you gave me back." Some people who are going to come back to you and say, "Well, I wasn't happy with what it was you sold me. I want my money back," and you're going to have to give their money back. The philosophy here — and this is what I thought was really ruthless — was that if that you're not making enough refunds, you're not selling hard enough. I've always been taught that when you sell anything to your customer, you need to make sure you've got it right there ready to deliver, and that you're managing every expectation, and you want to make sure that *there are no refunds at all*.

But in a ruthless mindset, if you're not making a certain amount of refunds, you're not selling hard enough, and you need to be happy to make those refunds consistently, so you're *still* managing the expectations of your customer and making them happy. That's extremely ruthless, because you actually go into it knowing, "I'm not going to make a lot of my customers happy. I'm going to make a whole lot more money because of it, because a lot of people are going to want my product and will buy it...

but I might have as much as 20% refunds on this individual item."

The whole concept of being bold and audacious (and, yes, ruthless) reminds me of the Solo-Flex story. For the first 20 years of his career, the guy who started Solo-Flex was a charter jet pilot who flew people from Los Angeles to Las Vegas and back. He worked for a company that had a rich clientele and he was probably making a good six-figure income, just taking the same small client-base from L.A. to Vegas so they could gamble. They didn't want to spend five or six hours to drive to Las Vegas, and didn't want to take a commercial flight. In any case, he got to know these people, and after a while they were all on a first name basis — but he was still making a six-figure pilot's income. **Many of these people were worth many tens of millions of dollars, and there were probably a couple of billionaires in the mix, too. One morning the pilot asked himself a simple question: "I wonder what it is, really, that separates me from these guys?"**

The answer was that these guys all had a certain level of audacity. They were just a little bit bolder than most people. It was in the way they carried themselves, the way they thought, the way they acted, the way that they took on everything in life and went after their dreams and whatever they wanted. **Once he realized that, his whole life changed. Within a matter of just a few years, he started the Solo-Flex Company and became a multimillionaire himself.** He was bold; he was audacious. You need to be that way, too. There's a famous book out called *Timid Salespeople Raise Skinny Kids*; it was written by Zig Ziglar's brother. I like that title, because it emphasizes part of what we're talking about with this ruthless mindset. **You have to have courage to take that next, audacious step: to advertise in a new, untested way, to reach out to a new segment of the market, to be willing to lose customers by making audacious claims. It's not an absence of fear. It's moving forward in spite of your fear, and that's really a lot of the secret right there.**

Here's something that helps me get in the ruthless mindset,

and it may be a good little drill for you, too. **Sit down with a pen and paper and think about your business, and some audacious, bold promises you could make to your consumer. Write those down, and be really outlandish; just write down whatever comes to mind. If you were the consumer, what could I say to you that would make you sit up and take notice?** Regardless of who else is in the field, regardless of the competition, they're going to want to figure out what it is you're talking about and want to pay attention to you. **Write those all down and then go back and weed out the ones that are literally impossible. It will be a good exercise to open up your mind. Focus on picking a couple of those, and then work them into your marketing strategies in some way.** Make sure, if it's audacious and bold, that you offer a guarantee so that any customer who's not happy with the results can definitely get their money back. Or offer some sort of a guarantee to ease the strain, in case it's too much for you to possibly deliver. Try to go out there and do everything morally and ethically, but try to make bold promises that make you stand out.

Pay Your Dues and Open Your Mind

One thing that'll boost your confidence and get you going courageously and boldly is working hard to develop your abilities. When you look at life, you can always tell those people or teams who've put in the time to be confident at what they're doing. Go out there and check the difference in the confidence level. **The people who've paid their dues, who've worked hard at being good at what they're doing, are out there taking on the world and accomplishing everything they want to accomplish, whether they're a courageous entrepreneur or part of a championship team.**

A ruthless marketer has to develop a mindset that continually motivates and encourages them to go out there and take those confident steps, to do those things they need to do to capture that market share. It all starts with study and learning and education: learning from the best, building a library that's filled with all kinds of books, tapes, and programs so you're learning from proven, successful people. There aren't actually a lot of people who go out and buy the books and programs they need to succeed. They'd rather sit down and watch a TV program every night and veg out. A ruthless marketer, on the other hand, goes out and grabs a book, reads it and gets some of these skills, or listens to a tape or studies a program to help him or her develop skills they need to succeed in their business. **It only takes one good idea, sometimes, to impel you into a marketing campaign that's going to return thousands, hundreds of thousands, or millions of dollars — but starting out, you usually can't tell what that idea is, or where it will come from. It all starts with education and study: paying your dues by doing some brain-work, then going out there and trying out some of the ideas you find, and maybe failing a lot more often than you succeed.**

On top of all that, you definitely need to keep an open mind. Nothing will close you down faster than thinking you already know it all, whether it's dealing with colleagues or clients or competitors. The main point I want to make about keeping an open mind is that you have to realize that your peripheral vision isn't as wide as you think it is. Many people go through life with such arrogance that they think they know it all; they know everything, and they don't need to go back to school to learn anything, or get a book or tape or a program, because they think their peripheral vision is so great — when in reality, they're looking through binoculars, and have tunnel vision about a lot of things. I've seen that over and over again — people who use arrogance to cover up their ignorance.

Even though a truly ruthless marketer may appear arrogant, that arrogance is usually backed up by study, research, and a firm understanding of marketing. **So focus on those things that help you become a better marketer, and develop the commitment, the dedication, the discipline, and the desire to learn. That's part of the ruthless mindset: making up your mind that you *don't* know it all, that you need to keep an open mind, that you need to expand your horizons so that that next ruthless** marketer doesn't catch up to you. If you're not putting in the time to learn and to study, someone else is.

Bad things happen to a businessperson who's been in business for a while and thinks they know it all. Here's something that many people like that do: they forget how to listen, to really listen, to teach themselves the value of and to understand the ideas and the opinions of others before criticizing those ideas and opinions. Because even when you know, deep in your heart, that someone doesn't know what the hell he or she is talking about, you can still learn what *not* to do. It's a good idea to keep your ears open — that's why God gave you two of them — and to teach yourself to value and understand the ideas and opinions of others before you criticize: to learn from them.

If you set things up in your daily life so you're expanding the things you need to expand and you're learning the things you need to learn, you're going to have an overall mindset that allows you to consistently think outside the box and do those things you need to do to succeed. **You'll have the courage to be bold in the marketplace, because your knowledge is grounded in solid, proven marketing strategies, and a mindset that keeps you on the cutting edge.** Now, it's not easy to stay there on the cutting edge. If you're going to be super-successful — year in and year out — you have to keep learning and growing.

That, right there, is your basic ammunition for becoming a ruthless marketer. That, and the fact that **you have to be disciplined: you have to know what you want and how to define your goals, and can't just expect great things to happen by chance. You have to put in the effort it takes to develop this kind of mindset, and simply believe you're going to be the best.** Last year, my buddy Chris Lakey's daughter, Ashleigh, was in a spelling bee. Every night she'd come home and talk about how she did in school that day. They practiced every day: they'd do these mock spelling bees, and she would constantly tell her Mom and Dad how she did, and about how she wanted to win. If she won, she got to go to the next level and participate in a spelling bee against a bunch of kids from other schools. Chris would tell her that if she wanted to win the spelling bee, she had to study better and harder than everybody else, and she had to continuously put in the effort to practice, to study the list of words they were going to be quizzed on. So she knew the parameters of the spelling bee — but she just wouldn't practice. She wanted it, but not bad enough to put the time in to practice, and so she finished second. Chris told her, after she finished second, that he was proud of her for finishing second — but that she couldn't be too upset when she didn't finish first, because she knew she hadn't put in the time it took to be Number One and to overtake that other person.

Now, that may seem a little harsh when applied to a little kid, but it's the same whether you want to win in kickball or in a spelling bee or in business. **If you don't put in the time and effort it takes to be Number One, then don't get mad when your competitors keep taking your business away from you. You have to put in the time, and you have to do more than say, "I want to be Number One in my marketplace." You have to do what it takes to be there. It's not just a matter of thinking it and writing down your goals; it's about doing what it takes to get to that top position in your marketplace.** You have to have that ruthless mindset that you're going to take as much business out of this marketplace as you can, and that you're going to be Number One. If you'll have that mindset to do that, then you can get there.

Let's use a sports analogy again. My colleague and friend Chris Hollinger used to be a basketball coach. I know for a fact, having spoken to him about it, that he saw players who weren't nearly as talented as others who ultimately performed better and more consistently than the rest. He told me how **he once coached a team that was made up of some extremely talented players; on paper, it looked like no one should have been able to touch them out on the court. But they really had to struggle in some games, simply because there were other teams that worked harder and had more discipline.** They had more dedication to the craft of basketball, and were more serious about coming together as a team than Chris' team was. Because the team Chris coached was so talented, the team members thought they could just walk out on the court and beat everybody with no problem. That's not always the case. As a matter of fact, they got second at State that year with a super-talented team that no one should have even been close to.

This only goes to show that having the right mix of skills and ability can actually be a downfall in some ways, because it makes you complacent sometimes. That's why you have to go back and be true to your craft and put in the time and the effort that it really takes to develop your talent even further. You see that in a lot of sports — and in a lot of businesses as well. You may not realize this, but the great Michael Jordan was *not* the best basketball player in his high school; he was good, but he didn't have all of the talent. By the end of his career, though, he'd trained so much and had worked so hard that he did. Tiger Woods is another example of someone who continued to work at his skills, to hone his craft into something extra special. **It works the same way with businesses, small or large. The people that continue to practice their skills, to work at their craft —whether it's marketing, or running a business as a whole — continue to make their businesses better,**

bit by little bit. It's an ongoing process increasing their sales and making their profits grow by leaps and bounds.

One of the things I find interesting about most business owners is that they seem to want to be *out* of their business desperately. Whenever five o'clock rolls around, they all want to leave. Whatever they're doing — whether it's plumbing or maintenance or carpet cleaning — they've started this business because they want a certain type of lifestyle, a certain type of income. They want to be self-employed, but they get buried in the day-to-day minutia of running that business, and so they all want to be out of it desperately. Now, one of the great things about being a ruthless marketer is that there's a lot of creativity involved; you've got a competitive spirit, and so you're always trying to do a little bit better and a little bit better. Instead of getting involved in the minutia of what cleaning products you're going to order this month, all of a sudden you've got your own little game going on. **Being a ruthless marketer is like creating your own game, where you're always trying to do better than the competition, or you're always trying to put out better marketing materials, or you're always trying to be a little bit better than everybody else. In doing that, you get to become more passionate about your business. You get to rekindle the passion about what you're doing.**

I think it's very important for you to step outside of that mindset of being the business owner. A lot of people, when they start a business up, fall into that business-owner mindset. You know: "I run a carpet cleaning business." Or, "I run a pet store." Or, "I'm a lawyer... an attorney." Don't fall into the trap. Instead, step into the ruthless marketing mindset where, "I'm a marketer." *That's* where the money is, along with the joy of the chase. **You're a marketer of whatever products or services you're currently promoting; you're not just a carpet cleaner. As I've said before, that seems like a tiny little difference on the surface, but there's really a big gap between being, say, a carpet cleaner and a marketer of carpet cleaning services.** Keep that in mind, and you'll be able to build a much larger, more successful business.

The Case of the Fan Company

I have a little story I wanted to tell about a case study I've been following now for a little while, one I've heard marketing coaches and other people talk about. **It regards a company that's within one of the most mundane industries you could ever imagine — but they've turned their business around by using ruthless marketing tactics, and by not being scared to try something different. This is a company that sells, of all things, great big fans.** I think it's a good example of a company that wasn't scared to do something different, to go out there and shake up the industry a little bit. The name of the company is actually "Big Ass Fans."

I'm not kidding. That's the reason I wanted to bring this case study to your attention, because... well, think about that name: "Big Ass Fans." This is a company that focuses their attention on developing large fans for cooling down warehouses and other big buildings. The reason I find this to be a great example of ruthless marketing is that somebody really had to be daring, really had to have some *cojones,* to go out there in this quiet little industry and change the company's name to what it is now. It was something really mundane before. But they listened to their customers — and **whenever their customers they saw their product, they tended to say, "Man, that's a big ass fan!"** You see, these fans are six feet or more across, and they have to be, since they sit up in the ceilings of really big buildings and keep the air circulating.

At some point, they took the plunge and changed the name of the company to Big Ass Fans from whatever it was before (I think it was something like Industrial Air Coil Flow Systems). Now, whenever you call the company, they'll answer the phone, "Hello, this is Big Ass Fans. How can we help you?" They're on the Internet; check them out. **At the time they changed their name, it was an action that was completely foreign to this industry. To do something like that that completely shakes up the industry and almost alienates you, because it's so odd. People think, "Man, those guys are weird. The name of their company is Big Ass Fans." But once they embraced the name, they got so much press and so much exposure that their company has since seen phenomenal growth.** They were in an industry where they were just plugging away with a plain name, and then they did something a little bit different and a little bit edgy and fun — and **they captured a huge percentage of the market share, just because they weren't scared to go out there and shake things up a little bit.**

Why Be Timid?

The Big Ass Fans example goes to show that **no matter how mundane your business is, if you're thinking ruthlessly, you can find an edge that'll let you get ahead.** Sometimes this ruthless marketing stuff is actually the *fun* stuff, because you're doing something different and exciting and new, and not necessarily worrying about what your competition is doing. It's all about being controversial. The key can be as simple as just shaking it up and making people question what you're doing. You might get some negative press — but sometimes negative press turns out to be good press anyhow. Be the innovator: I think that's another way to look at being a ruthless marketer as well.

Some people think that timid marketing is also safe marketing. Well, yes, that's true; but sometimes you have to be not so safe. You need to say to yourself, "Okay, I'm doing the same safe stuff everybody else is doing. What could I do, in terms of marketing, that would really push the envelope? **What could I do that would wake people up, slap them in the face and get their attention?" You might have to get a piece of paper and ask yourself that question, and jot down dozens and dozens of ideas. Go crazy. Just brainstorm. In doing that, you're really training your brain to have that ruthless mindset.** Because, really, that's what you're going to have to do: you're going to have to push the envelope, go beyond everybody else, and come up with that one idea that really makes you stand apart from everybody else. No, it's not safe. People are going to say, "I can't believe he's doing that!" But you really don't care what people say. What you care about are those numbers in your bankbook. Believe me, **it's the ruthless marketers, the people who are pushing the envelope, that are making a lot more money than all of the safe, timid marketers in those same industries.**

And here's something else about taking chances: it can be fun. As I've said again and again, most businesspeople are working *in* their business and not *on* their business. They're not having fun. I've got all kinds of friends who get up and go to work and they never have fun at all. But **ruthless marketing is one of the most enjoyable things I've ever done professionally, and I know many of my friends and colleagues feel the same. Done right, marketing is fun stuff! The energy and the ideas that flow out of my office, and the colleagues I talk to all the time, keep me busy enjoying life — and the next thing I know, 12 hours has gone by while I've been working on this marketing campaign, and now I can't wait to get it out there and get it going. Ruthless marketing is such a fun thing to do for a living, and it pays well if you're doing it right.**

That means you've got to get out of the employee mindset, as I've emphasized before. A lot of businesspeople just see their business as a job. You get to talking to them about their business, and you listen to the way they describe what they do, and it doesn't sound much different than most employees. There are plenty of exceptions out there, but with most employees, it's just a job; it's just something they do. It's the same with most business owners. They're involved in the day-to-day aspects of their jobs and they've got no ability to pull back away from it and see the whole thing as if it were more of a war or a sport or a game. I love the example of the Big Ass Fan Company, because you've got to do things that are aggressive and create wild and crazy guarantees and promises. You've got to do things that just blow people away! **Nobody is going to blow your horn for you. You've got to be the one that does it.** Truly ruthless marketers are so dedicated and focused on trying to do things that extract the largest amount of sales and profits out of their marketplace as possible, that they really don't give a damn about what other people think about them, or what other people say about them.

The older I get, the less aggressive I become, and it's really sad. I'm getting close to 50 years old now. I've been in business for 20 years, and I have to fight myself now to be more aggressive. What came natural to me ten or fifteen years ago I now have to do consciously. So I just want to say this: recently, I was scared about something that had to do with the marketing of a certain promotion. What I wanted to do was kind of aggressive and bold, but I was afraid of upsetting the people I was targeting, of turning them off. But then I realized just how unaggressive that was. **The phrase I want to give to all of our listeners now is something that has helped me so much, and here it is: "It doesn't matter who you piss off. It only matters who you *sell*."**

You can't do what I did. I was getting ready to make a bad mistake by playing it too safe, by holding back and being too conservative, by worrying too much about what other people were going to think about me, and how I was going to upset a few customers. **What I should have been focused on, and what I'm focused on now, is extracting the largest number of sales from that certain lead group of people who responded to an initial invitation — and forget about all the people who are going to be upset.** No offense to my good customers who may be reading this, but come on! The tendency is always to hold back more than you should. People are always worried, thinking, "Gosh, am I going to go too far? Am I going to push it too far?" Hey, the truth is, **no matter how hard you push it, you probably aren't pushing it far enough.** Too often, people go for bland vanilla marketing. They think they're trying to sell to everybody, so they try to be everything to everybody.

In doing that, you really don't create a strong basis for your business. In setting yourself apart and in making a stand, and in ticking people off, you're able to create a connection with those people who *do* like what you've got to say — or like whatever controversial thing you've put out there. They like the bold attempts you're making in your marketing. In doing that, you create better customers who are going to do more business with you. You're going to have a stronger business. Those are people who aren't going to run off to your competitors if they offer sales or discounts or things like that. **You have to change your mindset and say, "I'm not going to be everything to everybody. I'm going to be the best I** can for this particular section of the market and if other people don't like it, I'm not the best one for them. They need to find somebody else." If the Big Ass Fan Company hadn't thought that way, they'd still be some boring fan company no-one outside the industry had ever heard of.

No Doesn't Necessarily Mean No in Marketing

I compare just about everything that has to do with marketing with social situations. **Let's take dating, from a male perspective at least. There are plenty of guys, from the younger teens on up, who are very successful in the dating game. They sure don't let a "no" stop them. Fifteen "no's" just means they keep going at it from a different angle, until finally they get the answer they're looking for.** You have to be nice but aggressive to get the dates you want, and the same thing is true in marketing. I see so many people out there who are just aren't aggressive enough when it comes to marketing. They're weak. They wait around for business to come to them. They constantly take "no" for an answer way too soon. Whether it's in the dating game or in business, the people who do the best are a little aggressive. They may even keep asking the same person the same thing more than once. If you're a guy and you ask a beautiful woman to marry you, she's probably going to say no right away, especially if you don't know her well. In fact, maybe the first time she's going to slap you in the face, if you ask her too soon. But if you're really in love with her, you don't necessarily take that "no" as a final answer. I'm not talking about stalking her — just not giving up right away.

Here's a great example of something similar from the marketing field. My friend Kris Solie-Johnston once made a pitch to a large billion-dollar bank, and when they came back and said no, you know what? She didn't even hear "no." She heard, in her mind, "Not now." Think of it not as an N-O but as a K-N-O-W. It's not a "no;" it's an "I don't know enough to say yes." Make like you have selective hearing: that one word, "no," you just don't understand. You understand all other English words, except for that word one. "No" is not an option.

There are plenty of people who are very aggressive marketers who really won't accept a "no" as an answer. Because they're so passionately convinced that their product or service is right for their marketplace, nothing in the world is going to stop them. I think that's probably a better way of describing this. It's not about just trying to suck money out of people's bank accounts and trying to get people to hand over their money; it's about being so sure that what you have is so perfect for the people you're trying to reach, that they're just blown away by your total conviction, enthusiasm, and passion.

When you take that type of stance with your prospect or your customer, you're setting yourself up as an authority; you're basically saying, "Here's what you should do and here's why. I'm the expert." I've mentioned this before in other chapters. A lot of people will say "yes" if you just tell them, "Here's what you need. This is what you need to do." You get a lot more yeses that way than if you go out there and say, "I really think it would be good for you if you did this, because this will help your business." You don't want to do that: instead just state bluntly, "I think you should do this because if you don't, here's what going to happen, and you're going to regret it later. Do it now. I'll guarantee your results." That type of authoritative approach works well, as opposed to just going out there and stumbling around. **People respond to authority. It doesn't even have to be hardnosed, highhanded authority, either.**

Consider Oprah Winfrey, for example. Everybody knows Oprah's story and understands a little bit about her past, and how she rose to stardom, and how she comes across as a genuinely nice person who's happy to help people out. But that doesn't mean she's not in charge! She's got this Book Club, and I think it's interesting that **every time she says to read a book, millions of people run** out and buy it. She's not some literary expert: she's a woman who has a talk show. **But anytime she tells people they need to buy this or that book, they go out and do it, because she has authority and command over her audience base.** It doesn't matter what she tells them to do, either, because she's got so many loyal followers. She can say, "Everybody needs to go down to the store and buy this brand of orange juice," and a large percentage of her audience will go down and buy that brand of orange juice.

That's what you need to strive for with authority, too. If you take that stance and increase your credibility and build yourself into your consumer's mind as the ultimate authority, they'll pretty much do whatever you tell them to do. If you set out to grow that authority and build that rapport in order to use it in that capacity, well, that really is pretty ruthless — but it's very effective. **You want to build emotional bonds with your customers that are so strong that people are not only compelled to buy more of whatever you sell, but they'll feel guilty if they do business with one of your direct competitors.** I have such a relationship with a couple of the people I do business with — where it would almost be like cheating on a spouse if I was to do business with any of their competitors. How can you develop those bonds with your customers? That's the question that should keep you up at night.

Ruthless is as Ruthless Does

As I was doing research for this book, I went to my trusty Google to check out the definition of "ruthless." According to Google — which, by the way, I use for everything — "ruthless" means: pitiless, without mercy or pity. I started thinking about that; you know, if it's piti*less,* that means it would be the opposite of having pity. So, the opposite of ruthless to be full of pity for someone. So I went and looked up the definition of "pity" and Google told me lots of things about pity. But the best definition I could find was, "An emotion, usually resulting from an encounter with an unfortunate, injured, or pathetic person or creature." I

Developing
Marketing Systems:

1. You find out what
   works best
   through testing.

2. Then you expand
   those activities as
   far as possible.
   You do more
   testing to
   discover "how
   high is high?"

3. Then you focus
   on the areas that
   bring you the
   best results. You
   create
   procedures that
   make those things
   work
   automatically.

thought that was a pretty good definition of the word. But this is usually a term that's reserved for person-to-person encounters, or you and me on the street, or someone you see or hear about or read a story about.

I drew the conclusion from this that a lot of people get confused about "ruthless," and what we mean by ruthless marketing. Business is different from everyday life. Of course, in business your goal should be to serve your customers and make a profit. If you have pity on your competitors, you'll do all kinds of things to help them out. When someone steps foot in your door, you stop them and show them where your competitors are located, tell them why they should *not* do business with you, and why they should go down the street and do business with your competitors. Right? Well, of course not. That's preposterous — you'd never do that! No business would. Yet, without that ruthless mindset, that's exactly what you're doing. Every time you approach your customers with this lethargic attitude and think, "I'm just going to sit back and let the customers browse. I'm not going to do anything proactively," then you're pitying your competitors. **If you really are in business to make a profit, you've got to maintain the ruthless mindset that says, "Whatever it takes — legally, morally, and ethically — I'm going to get the most profits possible."**

It's the same thing with sports. In sports, your goal is to win. It doesn't mean you don't care about your competition as people; they're fellow humans. If you're watching a football game or playing in a football game, you don't try to kill the other guy. You just try to knock him down and do what you can to win the game within the framework of the rules. Your goal is to win, whether it's an individual competition like tennis or golf or whether it's football or baseball, where you're working within a team. In sports, the second place winner really is just the first loser. You can say, "Well, they still came in second place," if they didn't win — but that just means they were the first losers.

In business, **there really is a lot of money floating around out there being spent by your prospects and your customers. They're either going to be spending it with you, or they're going to spend it with your competition.** It's just a fact. Having a ruthless marketing mindset means that you play the game of business to win. You won't get all the money; no business ever does. But you want the largest share of your market's expendable income — the biggest share of the money they're spending — and you've got to have that ruthless mindset to get it.

I once heard someone say, "I don't want all my clients' and prospects' income. I just want all of their *disposable* income." That's the kind of ruthless mindset we're talking about. It's not about making your customers suffer or sending them to the poorhouse. **It's not about taking the money they should have spent to pay the car bill or the gas bill. It's just about getting the largest share of the money they're already spending on all that extra stuff they're going to continue spending money on.** You need to think about the term "ruthless" not as it applies to people, but as it applies to other businesses. If you can develop that ruthless mindset about your business competition, then you can succeed and you can be Number One in your market, and you can do the things that produce a winning edge in your business.

This morning I looked up the word "aggressive," and one of the definitions was: "making an all-out effort to win and to boldly and assertively move forward." I like that! It's about being on the offense — not on the defense — by staking your claim, by claiming your greatness. One of the guys **I admire a lot is the General Manager of my best friend's business. They've got over a hundred competitors in their local area, and it's not that big an area. He always says, "I have lots of competition, but I have zero competitors." I like that attitude. That's how I see it, too — and I see a lot of other people who have that aggressive kind of mentality. I think that business is not for the weak-hearted. You've got to be strong, you've got to be aggressive, and you've got to think of it as it were a war or a sport or a game.**

Nice Guys Really Do Finish Last

Although I do information marketing now, I often talk to people who run actual physical businesses — for example, veterinarians, or folks who have dry cleaning businesses. One of the things I get from them is they all want to be nice and have a community and not be aggressive or ruthless. Now, everyone advertises, but they all have this mindset of not going after anybody, of not being aggressive, of not competing against everybody else. All the ads in the Yellow Pages are exactly the same size. Everybody's trying to be nice. We're all trying to be friendly. We're all members of the Chamber of Commerce. Yeah, flowers and peace and all sorts of good stuff.

But that's not a way to run a business, and so I think **there has to be a shift in your mindset if you want to succeed.** What you'll find is that's how it is in most marketplaces. **Everybody believes they have competition, but no one is being competitive.** If you think that way, then you really have to develop a different way of thinking. When you understand not only that you have competition, but that you need to be actively competitive yourself, you really change your mindset. In most industries people aren't doing that. Your focus in business (as it's been said before) is to deliver great products and services you honestly believe in, to the most people possible, and to make as much money as possible. It's not to be friendly with your competitors. It's not to send Christmas cards to them and be able to say "Hi" to them in the grocery store. It's to be able to build a large, growing business. In many cases, that means being aggressive, being ruthless, and having that competitive mindset. It doesn't mean you're a mean person; it doesn't mean you're a bastard. Your relatives can still love you; your kids can still love you. But it does mean changing your mindset. And believe me, I've talked to enough business owners who have this friendly-friendly mindset that I do understand that it does take some effort to go from not wanting to rock the boat to becoming a truly aggressive marketer.

Let's go back to the sports analogy. One of the things I want to point out is that **you can never defeat an opponent you don't define.** You shouldn't think about your competition as, "I want to go out there and kill my enemy!" It's not like that at all, and that's what really makes it fun for me and for a lot of the marketers I know. We sit around every day thinking, "Okay, if I do this, I wonder what my biggest competitor is going to do? Or, if I do this, I wonder how they're going to react?" Because I'm thinking about their business and what they're doing and I'm thinking, "Man, I can really shake things up if I do this or that." That's what makes it fun! It's ruthless because you're thinking, "This is going to make these people sweat when I do this." You're not out there to say, "Here's the ball. Go run it into your end zone and make a touchdown." You don't want to watch people run by you! If you're in the game, you've identified your competitor. Then you're going head-to-head, and you're formulating plans and strategies that are going to help you get ahead and get into the end zone and make you all the money you want to make. That's how you gain market share.

For example, **here's a strategy. I was recently talking to somebody about this;** they're involved in an industry that's very chummy. They all put their arms around each other and say, "Let's go eat donuts together and get involved in these different community networks." **Even though they're competitors and they're all going after the same dollar, they get involved in these** little organizations and network meetings where they all sit around and drink coffee. What's funny is, the smart, ruthless marketers are joining those little committees and looking around, and learning what they can, and taking it back to their little laboratories (if you will), and putting it to work against their **competitors** — who have been lulled into this attitude of, "Oh, everything's happy and I'm sitting here drinking my coffee and eating my donuts and talking about marketing." The ruthless marketers are using those environments as learning environments to figure out what they can do next. My advice is, if you're going to join one of these things, don't do it just to become part of this little community and give away your best ideas. **Join it so that you can get in tighter with your competition and learn their insider secrets, so you can apply them to your business and help you gain market share on those same people.**

My colleague Chris Hollinger recently told me about an interesting experience he had. He went to a convenience store just right around the block, and when he pulled up in the parking lot, there were two plumber vans sitting there out front. One van just had the guy's name on it — something like "Joe's Plumbing." The other van looked a little nicer; it was a little cleaner, and maybe it was newer. The name on the side of this van was, "The Clog Father." The Clog Father van caught Chris' eye; it was a neat name. So he walked into the store, and there was a guy sitting over there sipping coffee out of a Styrofoam cup, in an untucked flannel shirt, playing Keno. The guy in the Clog Father shirt was buying something at the register and talking on his cell phone, conducting business. This guy had a nice shirt on that said "Clog Father" on it. Now, I don't know how successful both plumbers are; but who would you rather have come to your house and open your drains? **The Clog Father guy has done some thinking about how he wants to go about capturing his market share.** There's his competitor over there drinking coffee, playing Keno. That's all that Chris saw, and we don't know any of the details, but obviously the Clog Father has something going on. He's really considered what he's doing in the marketplace, how he's positioned himself, and how he presents himself. So you see, ruthless marketing can be done in every single business there is! You'd be surprised how many people are sitting out there, not really thinking creatively with their marketing. You may be one of them. Ultimately, to me, that's what ruthless marketing boils down to: thinking creatively about how you can go out there and capture that market share.

I think anybody reading this can take comfort in the fact that *most of your competitors are weak marketers.* Most of them are doing what I suggested in the beginning of this chapter: they're following the follower. They're doing exactly the same thing as all their other competitors are doing. Most people are like me. As I've mentioned before, I was a carpet cleaner for another company, and that's how I got into the carpet cleaning business. I started my own business because I was cleaning carpets for another guy, and then I decided I was tired of making him money and I wanted to be self-employed. But, basically, I was still just a carpet cleaner at heart.

Most business people are still employees, even if they're their own boss. I don't mean any disrespect to employees, but as I've shared in other chapters of this book, **the business you're in and the things that your business does — the products and services that you provide to your marketplace — are two entirely** different things. Most businesspeople still show up for work every day to punch their clock. They put in as little time as they have to put in, and then they leave. They're not thinking about this thing strategically.

Ruthless marketers, on the other hand, are constantly focused on getting as much business as they can. No company — except for an isolated few that got tangled up in personal or legal issues — ever went out of business because their sales and profits were too high. People go out of business because they get tired of working so hard for so little money. So you've got to be aggressive. **You've got to realize that there are a lot of forces working against you. There's the competition, and then there's the overhead. The markets are changing constantly. The solution to all these problems is to increase your sales and profits.** If you think aggressively and practice some of the ideas I've shared with you in this chapter, your business will continue to thrive and grow; your profits will continue to increase year after year.

Now, if you're struggling with the concept of competition and the "ruthless" way of going after someone else — maybe you're having a moral issue with it — then it might be better for you to try competing against yourself. When you're tracking the leads or customers you're bringing in on a weekly basis, ask yourself: how can you get more of them into your business? **Work to continually compete with yourself, instead of everybody else.** Compile your metrics and try to do better every week, and eventually it's going to get to a point where you're bringing in so many clients that the competition will be irrelevant. As you improve your business, one step at a time, the competition will no longer exist for you.

This is the End

Your job as a marketer and businessperson is to do as much business as you can with your customers, to penetrate as much of the marketplace as you can. **Every new customer must be won over, and sometimes you have to do something bold to attract**

them to you. Either you get their business or your competitor gets their business; it's your choice. When you study effective marketers, you'll see that they've got this ruthless marketing mindset. They're very aggressive. You need to do the same: **you've got to strike fast, strike hard, and strike often!** Stay in touch with your best customers. Keep trying to do things to do more and more business with them, and they'll be happy to give you more and more of their money.

That Brings Us to the End of This Small Book

Please keep this book close by and refer to it often. Take notes. Think. Find all the ways you can to use these powerful tips, tricks, and strategies, and in no time at all you will DOUBLE or even TRIPPLE your profits!

PLUS, as I also told you at the beginning of this book...

Your FREE business-building gift is waiting for you!

As I told you in the Introduction, I have just finished writing a new eBook, called: *"265 of the Greatest Marketing Secrets You Can Use to Dominate Your Market."* This Electronic Book normally sells for $27.95 — and is worth every penny. But for a limited time it can be yours — absolutely FREE — by simply going to my Web-Site and giving me your contact information.

Remember, I am giving you this $27.95 eBook for free because I have other business-building products and services that I would love to tell you about. So I'm more than happy to give you this brand new Electronic Book that gives you 265 of my greatest marketing secrets if you'll give me your contact information (which I will not give out to anyone).

Go to www.RuthlessMarketing.com/FreeGift and immediately download this very special Electronic Marketing book. And don't worry, although I <u>will</u> add your name to my mailing list and send you additional information, there is NEVER any cost or obligation for you to purchase anything else from me, now or in the future. This FREE gift will be my way of thanking you for taking the time to read and study this book.

MARKETING SECRET #40

The best marketing ideas for your business are evolutionary... It takes time.

- A marketing promotion must breathe... It must grow and develop... It goes through many stages before it is complete... You can't rush it too fast.

- In many ways, building a business is an artistic development that takes time, work, faith, creativity — and lots of thinking and intuition.

FREE GIFT: Go to www.RuthlessMarketing.com/freegift

www.ingramcontent.com/pod-product-compliance
Lightning Source LLC
Chambersburg PA
CBHW020206200326
41521CB00005BA/262